JIM RYERSON

SELLING BY
THE BOOK
TODAY

Timeless Wisdom in a
Referral-based World

Cover Design by Chris McMorrow
chris@mcmorrowdesign.com

Illustrations by Tim Kleyn
www.kleynillustration.com

© 2015 by James Ryerson. All Rights reserved. No portion of this book may be reproduced in any form, or by any means whatsoever, or stored in a retrieval system, or transmitted in any form or by any means (electronic, mechanical, photocopy, recording, scanning, or other -except for brief quotations in critical reviews or articles) without written permission of the author.

Ryerson, James, 1959 –

Other books by Jim Ryerson:

First 100 Days of Selling, A Practical Day-by-day Guide to Excel in the sales profession

First 100 Days of In-home Selling, The Secret of the One-call Close

ISBN-13: 978-1519651020

Team CertaPro,

We are embarking on a new generation of customers. As we aspire to transform the contracting space, we must embrace the changing landscape before us. The "uberfication" of our industry is at the forefront of this change and <u>Selling by The Book Today</u> gives all readers a leg up as the evolution speeds up. It really is quite simple. Not easy, but simple: live the "golden rule" and treat people the way THEY want to be treated.

Today having ratings out in the cyber-world for all to see is the new normal and CertaPro Painters understands how important it is to get and receive feedback from their customers and prospects. We welcome this information as a way to improve the experience for all that touch our brand. Those that embrace this referral-based thinking will reap the benefits by growing their businesses and truly delivering extraordinary experiences. The clock is ticking. Time is the new currency so I encourage you to embrace the change. It's not enough to ride the wave but to do so with the attitude that great people and great companies who embrace brand experience will be rewarded for their hard work.

CertaPro Painters and Sales Octane are "like peas and carrots". They just go together. We have had the good fortune to have worked with Jim Ryerson now for the past 4 years. He has left an indelible imprint on our Franchisees and Sales Staff. He has been instrumental through his wisdom and training on how to connect and ultimately get our prospects to say YES to CertaPro Painters.

In the pages to come you will get additional insights on how our future customers will buy from us, what matters most to them, and how to execute time honored principles in becoming referable. It's time.

Go Certa!

Michael Stone

President
CertaPro Painters

Table of Contents

Introduction .... *xi*

Chapter 1 15
Wave 1: "Where did my contact go?"

Chapter 2 19
Wave 2: Career-Hopping

Chapter 3 25
Wave 3: Customers Don't Need Salespeople Like Before

Chapter 4 31
Wave 4: "No one returns my calls!"

Chapter 5 37
Wave 5: More People to Connect With

Chapter 6 43
Wave 6: Time is the New Currency

Chapter 7 49
Wave 7: UBERfication

Chapter 8 53
Wave 8: "Who do I believe?"

Chapter 9 57
Impact 1: One Chance

TABLE OF CONTENTS

Chapter 10 61
Impact 2: Your Network = Your Net Worth

Chapter 11 67
Impact 3: "The Need for Speed" - (CRM) Customer Relationship Management

Chapter 12 77
Impact 4: Best Practices, On-boarding, & Selection

Chapter 13 85
Impact 5: Great Time for Great Companies and Great People

Chapter 14 89
You Must be Good...to be Great

Chapter 15 93
Likability Leads to Good and Then to Great

Chapter 16 99
Honesty

Chapter 17 105
Patience

Chapter 18 113
Humility

Chapter 19 121
Generosity

Chapter 20 127
Self-Control

TABLE OF CONTENTS

Chapter 21 137
    Speech

Chapter 22 147
    Listen

Chapter 23 159
    Knowledge

Chapter 24 167
    Connections

Chapter 25 177
    Wise Counsel

Chapter 26 187
    Organize

Chapter 27 199
    Plan Your Work

Chapter 28 205
    Work Your Plan

Chapter 29 217
    Next Step

Thank you! 219
References 220

Introduction

In 1989, while working for a research "think tank" in Ann Arbor, Michigan, I was exposed to the impact of the wave of change coming a quarter century in the future (2006). Often referred to in financial circles as the "Wall of Wealth," this massive shift would forever change the demographic landscape beginning in 2006. It was to be an orderly transition for decades to follow.

In 2002 after launching Sales Octane, a sales training organization, I began in earnest to address the implications of that demographic shift. In 2007, First 100 Days of Selling was published based on the fact that an enormous number of North Americans would begin retiring right about then and continue for 20-plus years. Retirements would mean replacements, promotions and incredible job movement between customers. New employees would be coming into organizations in need of new products and services.

In the world of sales the result would be a significant amount of new sales talent entering the market. Those new salespeople would benefit from the sales principles and techniques outlined in First 100 Days of Selling. It was a great plan, all based on research, and all driven by a dynamic you could not stop. It was a sure bet.

The best laid plans of mice and men often go awry
– Robert Burns

However, three unforeseen events threw this theory into chaos:

The impact of the dot-com bubble bursting from 1999 – 2001[1] began a mild recession and retirement savings began to shrink.

---
[1] http://en.wikipedia.org/wiki/Dot-com_bubble

Those thinking of retirement thought twice and decided to stay around a year or two while things shored up.

The dot-bomb was followed by the economic impact of September 11, 2001[2], which further cut into retirement savings. If you had a job, with benefits, it made sense to stay put and ride out the storm.

In 2007, concurrent with the launch of First 100 Days of Selling, the sub-prime mortgage crisis began and for two years we saw the financial industry meltdown and retirement savings melt with it[3]. Those of retirement age postponed their departure even longer.

So, it appeared the predictions of a non-stop departure leading to a multitude of new salespeople and new customers in new roles missed the mark as initially predicted. However, it is finally here and what was to be an organized transition is now a pent-up exodus.[4] Between the US and Canada alone the numbers are staggering. Between 7,000 – 11,000 people a day will retire over the next 20 years. The average is approximately 10,000/day (10K/Day).[5]

Ask anyone about their sales talent they will tell you how difficult it is to find qualified salespeople and how challenging it is to keep them. And we are just at the start of the wave.

---

[2] http://en.wikipedia.org/wiki/Economic_effects_arising_from_the_September_11_attacks
[3] http://en.wikipedia.org/wiki/Subprime_mortgage_crisis
[4] http://fivethirtyeight.com/features/what-baby-boomers-retirement-means-for-the-u-s-economy/)
[5] (Canada 1,000 a day) http://www.advocis.ca/forum/FMarchives12/FM-sep/caseStudy.html(US – 6000 – 10000 a day)
http://www.newsmax.com/Newsfront/RetirementCrisis/2010/12/27/id/381191/

Since publishing the second book in 2009, First 100 Days of In-home Selling, we have seen several new trends which are having an incredible impact on the sales profession. These trends, combined with the exodus of 10,000 people per day, create a Great time for Great companies and Great people. It will be a disaster for the rest.

In Selling By The Book Today we will:

- Cover the trends causing the shift in the sales landscape;
- Explain the impact for the sales professional and how to win in the new sales landscape; and
- Share several time-honored principles based on proverbial sayings (P.S.) that form the core of becoming referable.

It's time for Great people and Great companies to be rewarded for their hard work. Let's go!

Chapter 1
Wave 1: "Where did my contact go?"

Driven by 10,000 people retiring each day prospects, clients and salespeople will be changing jobs with alarming frequency. This is predicted to continue for another 18 years or more so prepare to see your prospects, clients and salespeople changing seats at previously unseen rates.

Here's how this plays out. Someone retires and it opens an empty seat.

You have three options with the empty seat:

1. Promote from within

In an effort to keep top talent and avoid the high cost of "onboarding" with a revolving door there is a tendency to promote from within. This can be good or bad depending on your current situation. For the salesperson it goes down like this: One day you are all set with your customer and the next day you are talking to someone you may have never met and who is now the new sheriff in town. This is bad if you have never met them and they desire to prove themselves by changing what their predecessor did, such as buy from you, so they start shopping your product/service.

However, there are two ways a promotion from within can be good:

> a) you have called on a prospective client for years in an effort to sell your solution but have not gotten anywhere and the internal candidate who is promoted may want to make a change from your competitor. Or
>
> b) you are currently selling to the customer and have a relationship with the new internal candidate or someone who can influence the internal candidate to continue with your solution.

This is not going to change so smart salespeople are adapting to the new environment.

2. Hire from the outside

This can be incredibly good or incredibly bad. Incredibly good would be the scenario of hiring a replacement from another company who is a current customer of yours and you find out about it quickly. BINGO. You may win as long as you connect with them quickly and make sure they increase the priority of switching from the current provider to your solution.

However, if you are the current provider you stand to lose if you have not secured support for continued use of your product or service prior to your champion leaving.

Incredibly bad would be the scenario of you being the current provider and they replace your contact/customer with a replacement from another company that uses your competitor's solution. Incredibly bad also means you are not aware of the transition of your contact leaving their role allowing someone else to slip in and make a positive first impression.

3. Eliminate the position

This is a third option when someone retires or leaves to take a job at another company. Following the dot-bomb, 9/11, the recession, the 2007-2008 sub-prime mortgage debacle, and the ensuing global impact meltdown, companies already eliminated roles in order to cut costs. At first they cut fat, removing team members who were underperforming, using the crisis to do what they should have done years before. But with each subsequent wave the cuts began to take the muscle out of their workforce. Currently, many companies are running lean and mean and have little to no fat. As a result, eliminating a position in the wake of a retirement or vacancy will become less prevalent for some time. So the current reality is most companies will replace individuals who retire and will either promote from within or hire from the outside.

Whether they promote from within or hire from the outside it opens up another seat, which will be filled and the changes continue.

This is the new reality. Salespeople and companies who understand this dynamic and act accordingly to take advantage of this shift will leave their competition behind.

Chapter 2
Wave 2: Career-Hopping

My Father worked two years for a company after graduating from college, then 37.5 years for the next company and then he retired. He worked two jobs over his entire career. Thus far, I have worked for three companies: 1 year, 25 years and now 13 years as of this printing and I believe this will be it for me. So, chances are I will have been at three jobs over my entire career. That was then but it is quite different now.

Enter the Millennials (born in the early 1980's-early 2000's). Future generations, beginning with the Millennials are far more comfortable changing jobs and with much greater frequency than previous generations. As of this printing, approximately 36% of the workforce has an average of two years experience in their current role and estimates are the average stay is now below 24 months.

While you may not see revolving doors being installed in every company, the fact of the matter is you will see your workforce and your client's workforce changing with increased frequency.

There is nothing inherently wrong with changing jobs frequently. Our intent is not to answer the question why do they change so often? Rather, we need to understand the consequences and implications of the frequency of change and how it will impact your sales team both externally and internally.

Externally – for the Salesperson

For 23 months you have diligently worked a key target account and are confident the customer will be giving you the contract within in the next 30 days. Your Vice President of Sales greets you every morning with the same question, "Have you heard anything yet on the contract?" and with confidence you respond, "Should be any day."

Then comes the call from your contact, the top level "decision maker" at the target account. She is leaving for another opportunity with a different company located on the other side of the continent. She is complimentary about the work you have done and lets you know she is not sure who will be taking over, but you will hear soon. She suggests you call into the main switchboard in a week. As you hang up the phone you have an uncomfortable feeling that aside from this primary "top decision maker" contact, who is now leaving, you do not have any significant connections within the target account.

In the months, years and decades to come, this will happen with alarming frequency, as the Millennials continue to make up a greater percentage of the customer base.

Internally – for Leadership

For 23 months your top salesperson, Kris, has diligently worked a key target account and is confident the contract will be awarded within in the next 30 days. You greet Kris every morning with the same question, "Have you heard anything yet on the contract?" and with confidence Kris responds, "Should be any day."

The following Friday morning Kris stops by your office, asks if you have a minute and closes the door. With no warning Kris shares the news that his contact is leaving for another opportunity with a different company located in another industry. There is a time set for later in the day to begin the process of reviewing their list of accounts (a spreadsheet with few details) but right now you, the VP of Sales, need to get your arms around the large target account.

As you review the details you come to the realization that Kris has a great relationship with the top-level decision maker but that is about it.

Then comes the call from the top-level decision maker at the target account. She is leaving for another opportunity with a different company located on the other side of the continent. She is complimentary about the work Kris has done and lets you know she is not sure who will be taking over, but you will hear soon. She suggests you call into the main switchboard in a week. As you hang up the phone you have an uncomfortable feeling that aside from this primary top decision maker contact, who is now leaving, you do not have any significant connections within the target account.

This will happen with greater frequency in the months, years and decades to come as Millennials continue to make up a greater percentage of your employee workforce.

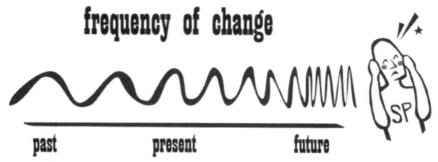

If you have had either of these situations even once you know the helpless feeling. In dealing with frequent role change, our energy needs to be focused on a couple of realities.

The Reality for Salespeople

If you have clients from the Millennial and subsequent generations, prepare to get more calls or emails informing you that your contact is leaving or, worse, already gone. Your customers will soon be installing a revolving door.

The Reality for Leadership

If you employ team members from the Millennial and subsequent generations, prepare for frequent transition. Prepare to bring on new salespeople with greater frequency. In many cases, these individuals will be new to sales or your industry meaning you will be doing a lot more training. Picture a revolving door installed in the sales department.

Chapter 3
Wave 3: Customers Don't Need Salespeople Like Before

My first job out of college was the role of a Purchasing Agent. It was short-lived as it became apparent the top salespeople on the other side of the desk were having greater financial success. However, those years as a Purchasing Agent gave me insight relative to the Customer-Salesperson relationship.

In the center of our purchasing office was an extensive collection of reference books, published annually, with all the providers for every possible commodity one would need to purchase. Whenever there was a need to purchase anything, I would head to the reference books to identify several providers. It was much like the Yellow Pages for manufactured components and larger corporate purchases. Remember the slogan for yellow pages? "Let your fingers do the walking?"

The next step in the process was to, "Let my fingers do the walking," by calling each provider on my list. I always spoke with someone, often a receptionist, and either left a message or was  transferred to another living, breathing, individual since this was before voicemail. After several back and forth returned calls and messages, "WHILE YOU WERE OUT" pink notes that littered the desk, appointments were set up with a salesperson from each company on the list.

A stream of salespeople would come in, share their capabilities, deliver their pitch, answer any questions I had and leave with the promise that I would get back to them. During this process I often met them face-to-face or at least spoke with them at length on the phone and began to experience their personality and style. With each proclamation of a feature, benefit or advantage I, as the customer, had to discern the validity and accuracy of the information from the salesperson and whether I trusted him or her.

Additional phone calls, conference calls and meetings took place and each time there was additional personal insight gained. Weekend plans and activities were discussed as the relationship grew.

The process continued as we narrowed down the possible providers creating what was referred to as the "short list." Those fortunate enough to secure a place on the short list were engaged again, either face-to-face or phone-to-phone, to provide additional insight, specifications and often pricing.

Occasionally site visits were planned to understand and see more of the provider's capabilities. During the site visit, buyers were introduced to additional contacts at the company and relationships grew. In many cases the providers were local or regional and it was often natural to have a common connection or to know someone who knew the salesperson or the customer. This created a transfer of trust from the connection to the salesperson.

Site visits frequently included a trip to a golf course, sporting event and at the very least included a breakfast, lunch, or dinner and possibly drinks. Whether we knew it or not or whether it was intentional or not, our relationships grew on a personal level.

Finally, the pricing, bidding and negotiation process would ensue with more face-to-face or phone-to-phone meetings. Through each step of this process I became more comfortable with the providers and narrowed the decision down to the final provider.

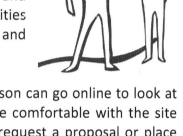

This process took weeks, sometimes months or even years. Throughout this process I got to know the salesperson. I met them, talked with them, ate with them, discussed our families, hobbies and even participated in recreational activities with them. I became sold on them and their company.

Now, it is a bit different. Today a person can go online to look at what options are available. If you are comfortable with the site you may look no further and simply request a proposal or place your order immediately.

You may look at the reviews, evaluate sites that provide a "top 10" list or reach out and select the "Contact Us" or "live chat" to ask a question.

Face to face and phone to phone has become the exception, not the rule. It is now possible to never speak with a salesperson.

This is known as disintermediation. Salespeople are becoming dis-intermediated or "dissed". The Internet has changed the game for salespeople. Customers have far more product knowledge a few browser clicks away than ever before. Search algorithm improvements have forever changed the ease of finding credible information of what is available to meet a need.

The Internet approach is fast, convenient and some would argue it levels the playing field by taking the personal influence out of the equation. You cannot be sold. It is possible to compare similar solutions, get the best value and move on.

At the very least customers are engaging with the salesperson later in the buying process, and as we will see in Wave 6 customers have less time once they do engage. In some cases, customers no longer think they even need a salesperson to gain knowledge. This is not going to change so smart salespeople are adapting to the new environment.

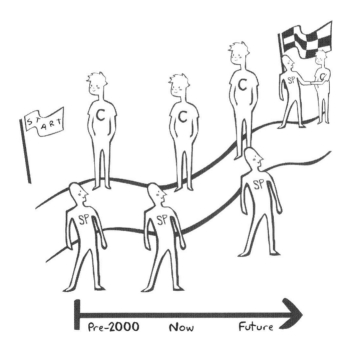

Chapter 4
Wave 4: "No one returns my calls!"

Let's look at two different daily rituals and their unintended consequences.

Ritual 1

When you walk into your office or look at your digital device, a natural irritation occurs when you see the blinking light indicating you have voice mail messages waiting. You have to pick up the phone, plug in your mailbox code and begin the dissertation on the time of the call and the number. Next comes the two to three minutes of often-disorganized chatter and, if the message is from a mobile device, much of it may be indiscernible. Often at the end of the message there is the rapid-fire telephone number, given once, forcing you to replay the message. This is if, you even

want to return the call or are still listening at this point. Four to five messages turn into eight to ten minutes of listening and writing the key points if you even listen to the complete message. If you don't listen to the message in its entirety, you still have to listen to the beginning, triage the fact it is not important before hitting the delete key. Eight to ten minutes, four to five times a day adds up and time is the new currency.

Ritual 2

You open up your e-mail and there are a bunch of new messages. The number of new messages will impact how much time you spend reviewing the subject line or the message before you delete, respond or file it. Think of this process as email triage. The more messages, the faster you delete. It is just human nature. You and I are getting more messages with every passing month. More messages equal faster deletions.

The term Unified Communications/Technology (UC/T) is a broad reference to the fact that phones are now becoming more about software than the copper wire device of old. It is now possible for voicemail messages to be converted to text using technology. A text message, along with the number of the caller, time, and length of message is sent via email to your inbox or digital application. No more pressing buttons and listening to disorganized chatter. No more pressing the replay key five times to discern the 10 digits of the phone number they rattled off. No more walking into your office and getting sick at the sight of the blinking red "message waiting" light. No more anxiety at hearing "you have 6 un-played messages" when you sign into your voicemail. It is now possible to have an email of the transcribed message. It's lovely. As a matter of fact, once you begin using this technology you will hardly ever answer the phone again, and neither will your customers.

The Unintended Consequence

Salespeople who leave voicemail messages that are disorganized, inarticulate, not relevant or "cold" will never be heard from again. They will be one email delete key away from obscurity. No one wants to return a call from someone you can't understand clearly. No one wants to return a call from someone who talks too much. No one wants to return the call from someone who is not relevant. And, ultimately, no one will return the "cold" email (think cold-calling).

Why Sounding Great No Longer Matters

Even the salespeople who are organized and articulate will lose the opportunity to have the prospective customer hear their smooth vocal inflection. The reason it was named "voice" mail was because your customer would hear your voice. Your vocal inflection, if good, was a strength when leaving voicemail messages for prospective customers. They heard your voice and made a number of positive conclusions. However, in the absence of any visuals, because it's the phone, and vocal inflection, because it's transcribed to text, you have lost about 85% of your strength.

Gets Worse

Going back to the discussion about email, with unified communications the number of emails will increase. Emails now will include voicemail that has been transcribed and sent as email. As a result, your customers will triage more quickly by deleting irrelevant email.

It is possible that customers will get rid of voicemail all together as Coca-Cola did in late 2014. Instead, corporate headquarters encouraged their workforce to find alternative methods to connect.[6]

---

[6] http://www.bloomberg.com/news/articles/2014-12-22/coca-cola-disconnects-voice-mail-at-headquarters

One last thought. When was the last time your son or daughter responded to your voicemail if, in fact, they have not already turned off their mobile phone voice mail. This is a harbinger of what is to come, as this is your future customer.

Smart salespeople are taking note of this evolution and putting a plan in place to leave their competition in the dust (or, more accurately, in the email trash).

Chapter 5
Wave 5: More People to Connect With

The "Good Old Days"

In the past there was often one person, a single point of contact, who made, or at the very least drove, the decision to acquire your product or service.

We called on the single point of contact, took them breakfast, lunch, dinner or cocktails. They attended sporting events with us and we took an interest in them.

It was very simple and clear as long as you had a great relationship with the single point of contact. They made or drove the decision in your direction and you were set. Because the single point of contact rarely changed companies, and often rose in power through the ranks, this was a beautiful situation. Hence the reason this period is often referred to as the "Good Old Days."

The "Great New Days"

Single point-of-contact decisions are rapidly becoming committees, multiple stakeholders and a consensus approach. If your customers, your product, or your service aligns with any of these eight characteristics, then committees, multiple stakeholders and a consensus approach is in your future, if it's not already a reality:

1. The problems; meaning the problems or needs your customer is experiencing and/or the solutions your product or service addresses

are ill defined, or there is disagreement about how they should be defined by other stakeholders.

2. Several stakeholders have a vested interest in the problems and are interdependent meaning they want their voice to be heard or they must win!

3. These stakeholders are not necessarily identified as a cohesive group or organization meaning not everyone is on the same page or singing the same tune.

4. There may be a disparity of power and/or resources for dealing with the problems among the stakeholders. Stakeholders may have different levels of expertise and different access to information about the problems. This pretty much defines every company in the world...so you now have at least one situation where consensus is real with your customer!

5. The problems are often characterized by technical complexity and scientific uncertainty. If your product or service is complex, this means you.

6. Differing perspectives on the problems often lead to adversarial relationship among the stakeholders. How often do you observe stakeholders arguing their position or taking sides?

7. Incremental or unilateral efforts to deal with the problems typically produce less than satisfactory solutions. What they are using or doing today is not working.

8. Existing processes for addressing the problems have proved insufficient and may even exacerbate them[7]. This is not their first rodeo and it's becoming a goat rodeo.

---

[7] Burgess, Heidi and Brad Spangler. "Consensus Building." Beyond Intractability. Eds. Guy Burgess and Heidi Burgess. Conflict Information Consortium, University of Colorado, Boulder.Posted:September2003
<http://www.beyondintractability.org/essay/consensus-building>.

When looking at the above list there is better than a 90% chance your customers identify with at least one and probably several of the situations noted. If it is not the customer, then it is likely your product or service will align with at least one of the situations noted. The only caveat may be if you sell into the home environment arena. However, even when selling to a family unit there may be a high probability of multiple stakeholders such as spouse, family member, trusted advisor, friend, or neighbor.

My guess is every one reading this book has come to the conclusion they have encountered at least one of the situations noted that drive the need for consensus!

Generational Shift

Add to this the Millennials' desire for increased engagement and collaboration in decisions impacting their world. The new reality is there are now, and will continue to be, more people than ever to connect with, engage and influence during the sales process. Gone are the Good Old Days of a single point of contact.

The bullet points in this section were drawn from: Barbara Gray, Collaborating: Finding Common Ground for Multiparty Problems, (San Francisco: Jossey-Bass Publishers, 1989)

Multiplicative Impact of Additional Stakeholders

As additional stakeholders join the committee to decide about you and your solution, the impact is not linear but rather

multiplicative. Metcalfe's law [8] illustrates how lines of communication increase exponentially with each additional stakeholder. P*(P-1)/2. People*(People-1)/2. 28*(28-1)/2 = 28 lines of communication.

---

[8] http://en.wikipedia.org/wiki/Metcalfe's_law

Casual conversations take place that create challenges for the committee and the sales professional. Since you are outside the organization you will have the challenge of navigating this maze.

In the previous illustration, the sales professional is calling on a customer committee comprised of seven stakeholders. The lines of communication total 28 using Metcalf's law. The plot thickens as those stakeholders band together and factions develop to posture for their choice of solution and provider; think of these relationships as little fiefdoms. The sales professional now has to manage communication between these fiefdoms, dramatically increasing the lines of communication and possible outcomes.

When the calculation is made to include all of the stakeholders in the process, including sub-groups which band together, the complexity evolves to over 255 possible outcomes. Outcomes = (2^People)-1 or in this example Outcomes = (2^8)-1 = 255 possible outcomes.

It may feel a bit like playing a game of Whack-A-Mole, because about the time you deal with one stakeholder or sub-group another raises an issue.

Chapter 6
Wave 6: Time is the New Currency

The digital revolution began when the Internet/World Wide Web (www) came on the scene and access to information served as a major efficiency improvement. Communication was accelerated and life was good.

Email eliminated the plethora of WHILE YOU WERE OUT messages as communication transitioned from phone to email. This could not be better for efficiency (unless you were the salesperson who sold WHILE YOU WERE OUT pads of paper).

Companies ran to develop websites validating their relevancy. Before long the website became a clearinghouse where information could be posted to help existing and potential customers with efficient access to information and knowledge. This previously required laborious phone calls and waiting for the mail. Life became ever better.

Email marketing kicked in to provide a cost-effective, efficient and tailored method to keep your company in front of customers and prospects. This was great for companies and even consumers enjoyed the "deals" often included with the marketing blast.

Search engine optimization became more refined. Anyone with a basic understanding of a computer could find anything they wanted on the Internet.

Social media and social networking came on the scene as a way to keep in touch and reconnect with all your "friends." Old relationships were rekindled. Memories were shared with others efficiently and in many cases in real-time. It was beautiful.

Blogging and Tweeting provided an opportunity to share your real-time position and knowledge about issues that mattered to you. Those of the same mindset could then follow your statements as a way to refine their thinking. What a great way to share meaningful information!

It was a Time Saver Until

Email soon became overbearing, as everyone who was copied on the original email would hit the dreaded "REPLY ALL". With every reply, the email inbox began to fill. Emails were often used as a way to take a passive strike towards another party regarding your position. Picture someone lobbing a grenade over the wall and running for cover. Team members hid in their cubicles sending emails to other team members a few feet and one partition away. Voice and Visual was lost to a series of "Reply All" counter positions. Copies of The Art Of War by Sun Tzu were analyzed as strategies were developed for your next electronic salvo. Email soon became a source of anxiety and tension as hours were spent trying to stay ahead of the inbox.

Websites moved from helpful to a cluster of hyperlink buttons akin to a series of rabbit holes you could not get out of. In an effort to provide everything anyone could ask for companies did just that and the complexity of websites grew. Recall the heralded move by Google to provide one single place to enter what you were looking for. It should have been a roadmap for others but for whatever reason it never became mainstream.

With the improvement in search engine optimization not only could you find anything you were looking for, you were also drawn to those you were not looking for. Minutes turned into hours of mindlessly drifting down the flowing current of hyperlinks as you traveled deeper down the rabbit hole.

Email marketing started to tip the scales and increased the volume of information cluttering the In-Box. The well intentioned, "I'll just take a quick look", and subsequent click of the hyperlink often resulted in more time than initially intended.

Social media and networking, once a noble way to connect with friends and family, suddenly became a non-stop barrage of interruptions as postings grew on our digital devices. Many of the updates became insignificant events that if you had not been notified, would have no impact on your life. Worse, in many cases the quick view of the update becomes irritation and anxiety at the fact YOU are working and EVERYONE else seems to be on a beach somewhere.

It all started out great. Each item, in and of itself, is a massive improvement over the alternative. Frankly, if asked the question, "Jim, if you could only take one item with you on a deserted island, what would it be?" My answer would depend on one thing. "Would there be a power

generator with me?" I would not want to try to get along without my digital device and my guess is you are the same. And it is always with us.

The separation between your work and your personal time is blurred, if not completely gone. Work follows us via our digital devices as we attempt to stay ahead of our workload. We open our device to find something personal and are inundated with work. All of this combines to overload customers. Discretionary time to sort through the options is becoming increasingly scarce. As average users, customers spend 3.5 hours per day on-line. This is time they don't have to meet with you. Time is the new currency for them and for you.

Chapter 7
Wave 7: UBERfication

UBER is simple. You are in a city and need a cab to travel several blocks (New York City) or several miles (Atlanta). You can stand and flag one down (New York) or stand and wait and wait, and wait (Atlanta).

When the cab finally arrives, you jump in and there is that question, "Will you be paying cash?" which is meant to make you uncomfortable if you were planning to use a credit card.

The quality of the car, cleanliness of the inside, demeanor of the driver and aroma of the interior is a total gamble. When you get dropped off there is the final issue and often discomfort around the tip. Then came UBER.

UBER allows you to identify where you are and where you are going via the Geo-positioning built into your mobile device. Within seconds "drivers" bid against each other in a variation of a reverse auction. You get a TOTAL price, tip included, and because your credit card is already in the APP there is no question of "Will you be paying cash?" When you arrive at your destination your transaction is complete.

If the UBER trend stopped at cabs this chapter would be finished. But it will not stop with transportation. The home improvement industry (think carpet cleaning, maid service, window washing, painting and carpentry services) is in the process of being UBERfied. You go online and tap in what you are looking for. Pre-approved area contractors respond in a matter of minutes and you, the buyer selects your provider.

If you believe you are immune, think again. The question is not if this is going to happen to your product or service, but when and how. Regardless of whether you are in a business-to-business environment, business to consumer environment or online environment you will be UBERfied.

Back to the UBER cab scenario. IF you jumped in an "UBER car" and the experience (think aroma, demeanor of the driver, speech issues, condition/cleanliness of the car, etc.) was not up to your expectations, you have an opportunity to rate the driver and experience. This information is provided to UBER. If there is an unsatisfactory rating the driver will need to go through a complete evaluation process to get back on the list.

Only the best will survive being UBERfied. Alarming? Maybe. But this is also GREAT news for GREAT companies. GREAT companies will benefit from this shift in the marketplace and they are putting the systems in place to ensure they are Great!

Chapter 8
Wave 8: "Who do I believe?"

I travel about 100 days a year. Oftentimes I eat by myself so I can write or catch up on the emails and work that piled up while I was speaking at the convention. When I am in a new city I like go to several restaurant rating APPs or Sites online to evaluate my options for dinner. Initially these were quite reliable. The comments were an honest, accurate evaluation about the food, atmosphere and experience. When the review stated "the most authentic Italian food I have had outside Italy," it was very reliable. A 5-star rating meant a 5-star dining experience awaited me that evening. In the early rounds of the ratings process, regardless of the service or product, the comments and ratings were honest and reliable.

Then, as time went on a disturbing trend evolved. Highly rated restaurants turned out to be anything but amazing. Reading through the comments one person would be raving about "the most authentic Italian restaurant ever visited…just as good as being in Italy," and right below was another comment "worse Italian food ever, I will never go back!"

As I reviewed the ratings I now wondered about the source. Poor service and negative reviews may have been posted by a competitor out to discredit a worthy provider. Positive ratings are often the result of a concerted effort by the employees, friends and family members providing exceptionally positive postings and ratings for their restaurant. There is now so much conflicting information on these sites one begins to ask the question, "who do I believe?"

In the LOST INTERVIEW video series, Steve Jobs made the insightful observation, "The smallest company in the world can look as large as the largest company in the world with the web." This has proven to be accurate in terms of scale of company and the way the web has leveled the playing field. However, with author-controlled websites, and the reliability of the claims made, you could change the word "smallest" for the word "worst" and "large/largest" for "great/greatest" and the above statement remains accurate.

The WORST company in the world can look as GREAT as the GREATEST company in the world with the web. We could even reach a bit further and change the word "company" to "person"— The WORST person in the world can look as GREAT as the GREATEST person in the world with the web. It's a slippery slope. So, who do you believe?

There is so much conflicting information available and it is difficult to sort through and find the truth. Impressive, flashy websites optimized to grab you when you search for information often cause us to wonder about the validity of the claims being made. Once you find a reliable provider you are slow to look elsewhere unless the reliability changes. The time required to look elsewhere in the ever-expanding web is weighed alongside the savings you would gain.

Who can you believe? The answer is quite simple. Someone you Trust.

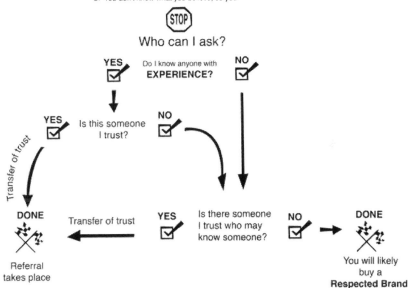

Chapter 9
Impact 1: One Chance

Your customers have far less time today and will continue to have less time in the future. This translates to less time for you and any other option they are considering. This can be good news or bad news. Since they have less time to review alternative options, if you make a positive first impression, you may be able to move them away from evaluating other alternatives. You never get a second chance at a first impression.

Your customers often engage with you farther down the road in the buying process. This trend of engaging later in the buying process will continue. In the old days you were engaged early in the process as the customer began to gather information about their needs. Not any more. This is driven by a lack of time and the availability of information and on-line research. When the customer finally decides to engage with you they have already done their homework. They often come with specific and challenging questions and once you get in front of them, you must be relevant.

You were contacted for a reason. Given the fact the customer has already completed their initial research, something caused them to reach out to you. Seldom will you have a customer reach out for basic information because it was already provided to them on your website. At the same time, the initial inquiry from a customer routinely comes in forms other than a telephone call, such as an email or a contact request on-line. This is great news for the sales professional. You can now figure out what they heard about you, why they called you and how you can leverage your first conversation!

Qualify Early and Qualify Often

In the book, *Let's Get Real Or Let's Not Play*, Khalsa and Illig masterfully illustrated the fact top sales professionals closed at a higher rate when they spent more of the initial sales process qualifying and advancing the conversation vs. jumping to the presentation/price/proposal.[9] Since the first communication is often in the form of an email, contact us form, or voicemail message, the sales professional has at least some time to thoughtfully respond with qualification questions to provide relevance. In some cases, if the customer has incorrect information which could result in a poor decision, we may even challenge the customer during this initial communication.

Customers Reward Relevant Questions

People love to buy but they hate to feel like they are being sold. Remember, the customer reached out to you for a reason. They want to buy something. They called you versus your competitor. Someone they know and trust may have recommended they give you a call, or they saw something in their research leading them to believe you are relevant. They want to buy but they do not want to feel like you are selling them. Make the most of your first impression by asking relevant questions or this may be your last encounter.

What About Prospecting and Unsolicited Calls?

While cold call prospecting will become increasingly difficult with the Unified Communications movement the same reality applies. You never get a second chance. You must make a connection during the prospecting process. An unsolicited call is met with

---

[9] *Let's Get Real Or Let's Not Play*, Mahan Khalsa and Randy Illig, page 27 Penguin Books, Franklin Covey 2008

skepticism and distrust. Add the fact they can block your number/email address if they were not impressed with you the first time.

So how do you make a positive first impression? Four words: Relevant, Trustworthy, Experienced and Brief.

Chapter 10
Impact 2: Your Network = Your Net Worth

For the Sales Professional

Your network will determine your net worth in a referral-based world. The old adage, "It's not what you know, it's who you know" is just that, old.

It's WHAT You Know...

In a referral-based world what you know, your knowledge, is important. Your customers have already obtained information about your product/service on the Internet long before they connected with you. Their committees now include stakeholders from various backgrounds who also researched your product/service. Customers engage you later in the buying process, often after they have discussed your product/service with the stakeholders. When they finally engage with you they have more knowledge than ever before. So what you know is important or you will become irrelevant.

WHO You Know…

Who you know is also important. With 10K/Day retiring and career-hopping as the new norm, contacts will be changing roles and companies with such frequency it will make your head spin. Your network of contacts has the power to help you leap past the competition. By following your network to new opportunities you bypass the traditional prospecting routine. With a robust network you can proactively engage customers as they begin the buying process. In some cases you can proactively engage customers before they even identify a need.

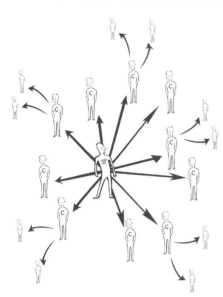

And WHO KNOWS You!

There's one more element in a referral-based world; Who knows you? The goal of the sales professional is to circumvent normal channels and secure relationships proactively. This strategy will only work when others are aware of you and the value you bring to your network of customers. As your network grows and you become more knowledgeable and relevant, you

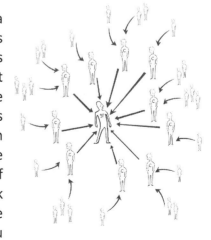

will be able to engage with customers while your competition is stuck in Unified Communications Purgatory. The sales professional is taking a position right now as the knowledge leader and proven performer worthy of the next referral. It will be the only way in a referral-based world.

Your Organization's Network Increases Your Reach

It is essential to leverage the network of your entire organization. In this early phase of the evolution to a referral-based world, it is a numbers game. Your ability as a sales professional to proactively identify a connection begins with a robust network.

Over time you will divide and conquer. Over time you will become more selective as you build your referral stream. Over time you will hyper-focus on your ideal customer. But it is essential that you start with growing the network.

For Leadership

Your entire corporate team's network is soon to become your net worth. With 10K/Day retiring, and career-hopping as the new norm, your organization will be impacted by team members coming and going. Add growth into the mix and it increases the speed of change.

With all of the coming and going, it is essential to capture and maintain your organization's network of contacts. This is not directed towards existing customers. In most cases their contact information is already captured. If not the sales person is at risk of network bankruptcy. It is essential to capture the expanded reach of every network contact secured while team members are part of your organization.

Think of their network as if it were a patent. Patents are typically co-owned by the team member who created the intellectual property and the organization they work for at the time. Contacts are intellectual property. It is your responsibility to put a system in place which helps both the sales professional utilize their network to grow their sales and to maintain the data in the event of a change. It's a win–win. In a referral-based world those network contacts have a value and that value will soon define the net worth of your organization.

So what does this look like?

Chapter 11
Impact 3: "The Need for Speed" - (CRM) Customer Relationship Management

More Touches

The sales professional can no longer keep up with a pen, paper and a calendar, not even an electronic calendar. There are now more prospecting calls, email attempts and touches along the way to secure a conversation with a customer.

Unified Communications will continue to develop barriers for the sales professional that equate to additional steps in the process regardless of the stage in the sales cycle. You will have no other choice but to put together a system to manage the process efficiently and effectively until your referral network is in place. Once the referral network is in place the system will seem less oppressive.

Trust Erodes

Sales professionals do what they say they will do. They call or arrive when they say they will. They follow up when they say they will. They send information when they say they will. With increasing touches and higher customer expectations the standard pad of paper or calendar cannot keep pace. Keeping on top of those touches without a robust Customer Relationship Management system and doing what you say you will do are often at odds with each other.

Finding the L.I.N.K.[10]

As your contacts and referral network grow, pulling the pieces together will continue to increase in complexity. Where did the lead come from? Who knows whom? Who do I know that knows the customer? What do I know about the customer? What is their Line, Interest, Need, who and what do they Know? Finding the L.I.N.K. requires data and data requires a system.

Where Are They Now?

10K/Day and career hopping means you have to efficiently and dynamically change contact information as your customers, contacts and referral sources transition from one organization to another.

UNDELIVERABLE

Prepare to receive more electronic auto responses with the term UNDELIVERABLE. Your customer is no longer there! Contact information for customers must remain up to date in order for Drip Marketing campaigns and links with Social Media campaigns to work. Several years back during a conversation with a customer we were discussing the increase in UNDELIVERABLE email responses to their Drip Marketing campaign. I typically counsel clients to make sure to capture those emails and get them back to the sales team. This is often an indication of a change at the prospect or customer which could mean another lead. However, in this situation the head of I.T. was all too excited to share they already had a process in place. The customer responded, "No problem. We put a system in place to sort out the undeliverable emails and remove them from the system so

---

[10] L.I.N.K. - First 100 Days of Selling

the salespeople won't be bothered." Ouch! Good intentions, however, an entire generation of referrals and leads were eliminated in the process.

I Need You to Cover These Customers

With new sales talent showing up on an ever-increasing basis, the contact information must be easily transferred to the new sales professional. Sorting through a Rolodex, stacks of business cards, spreadsheets, computer files or pads of paper, if you can even find them, is both inefficient and ineffective. In most cases the good information is already gone and possibly with your competitor. This is setting up the next sales professional for failure.

Good News and Bad News

Because customers wait longer to reach out and engage you in their buying process, you have less visibility to forecast. The sales funnel looks more like one of those large green straws from Starbucks than it does the traditional funnel. Sales forecasting needs to be real time so companies can plan their operation accordingly. Real time requires a dynamic CRM system. Your only other option is to call and email all your sales professionals, have them stop selling for the day, review their notes and spreadsheets, update the information, send it back to you and then you will take time away from coaching and leading to summarize the results.

Typically, about the time the new forecast is complete you have already received several emails and calls from your sales team regarding a win or loss that impacts the forecast. This is both inefficient and ineffective and takes everyone away from selling.

One and Done

Time is the new currency for the salesperson. Systems to capture information and reduce duplication will free up the sales professional to sell. By eliminating redundancy in the process of pre-call research, pre-call planning, strategy development, prospecting, appointments, note-taking, follow up and the next step, you free up their time to sell. By putting the information in one time the rest of the system will update automatically. Requiring the sales professional to put the same information in multiple spreadsheets or legacy systems is both inefficient and redundant. One and done. Back to selling.

"I already told you!" or, worse, "I already told them!"

Time is the new currency for customers. They have little patience for a salesperson who can not locate information previously shared. It is essential to capture every detail of every customer interaction and have it a click away. Add in the fact customers often delay for months, quarters and even years due to their organization's lack of revenue forecasting and the situation is made worse.

Everyone on the Same Page

Team selling is a key sales strategy moving forward. As more of your team members are involved in the sales process they will need access to real-time information about the opportunity and customer. As changes occur with your customer, those updates must be made in real time to keep the team on the same page.

Martha Stewart was Right

Each issue of Martha Stewart's magazine, *LIVING*, includes a calendar with tasks to perform that month. When I first saw the calendar years ago I thought that's insane. Who plans out to scrub gas grills and clean the potting shed? But the thing is, I should. Usually I react to a project under pressure. Company comes over and when I open the gas grill it appears something has taken up residence. After looking for pruning shears for an hour I decide to just take the rest of the day and clean out the potting shed. These routine activities become interruptions versus planned execution.

There are always routine activities the sales professional should do in a consistent manner and without a lot of thought. Providing a system to efficiently capture those routine best practices will improve their time management and ensure they do not become reactionary. It also positions your new sales talent to enter a sales system that leverages the knowledge of your top performers.

R.I.P.

Pads of paper or a day planner no longer capture and share data in an efficient manner. Given the additional number of touches in the sales process, the sales professional must be equipped with a Customer Relationship Management system that increases access to information and supports the sales process in an efficient and effective manner. For years organizations have pumped billions into ERP (Enterprise Requirements Planning) initiatives. The predictions are that in 2017 worldwide investment in CRM systems will eclipse spending in ERP.[11]

---

[11] http://www.forbes.com/sites/louiscolumbus/2013/06/18/gartner-predicts-crm-will-be-a-36b-market-by-2017/

It's Coming. Are You Ready?

Step 1 – Intent matters. It's not about being right, it's about getting what you want. The guiding principle with any CRM initiative must be to help the sales professional become more effective and efficient. If the CRM system does not make them more effective and efficient it will not work because they will not use it. If the sales professional sees the benefit for them they will use it and you get what you want. Win-Win.

Step 2 – Develop a need statement. Chances are this list will be outdated as soon as this book comes off the printing press. But at least it is a place to start:

- Facilitates, aligns with and drives the sales process
- Customizable – every sales process is different
- Support options – you will need support, plan on it
- Training needs
- Mobile
- Cloud-based
- Platform agnostic (iOS, Microsoft, Google/Android, etc.)
- Integration with other legacy programs/software/systems
- Allows add-ons (example: LinkedIN, blogging, Twitter, other social media)
- Scalable – you can start small and the system can grow with you
- Allows import of data (leads, data, customer lists, order information, etc.)
- Forecasting – easy for users to generate a forecast
- Automates tasks to eliminate manual repetition
- Funnel management; status, insight, etc.
- Contact notes and history

- Key activities to measure – what gets measured gets done
- Portability - easy to transfer information from one person to another
- Easy to pull a summary of the customer situation
- Drop downs – key steps in the sales process do not require typing each time
- Measurements/Reports – Inspect what you expect

Time is the new currency for leaders. For the CRM to work for leadership and sales professionals alike, the CRM must easily provide the accurate reports and information you need, when you need it.

Step 3 – Revisit Step 1 and confirm that the Need Statement aligns. If not, revisit Step 2.

Step 4 – Map out your sales process. Every step, every detail must be defined visually. Identify the points in the sales process where your sales professionals must enter information. For more information go to "www.salesoctane.com" and select SalesMap™.

Step 5 – Revisit Step 1 with the sales team while standing in front of the SalesMap™. If everything aligns with Step 1 and 2, move to Step 6. If not, do not even think of moving forward.

Step 6 – Evaluate CRM options using your Needs Statement and the SalesMap™.

Step 7 – Once you have a list of possible providers, have your top sales professional, the one you cannot afford to lose, use a Beta of each possible solution with Step 1 as your guide. If everything aligns, move forward to Step 8. If not, please, I beg you, do not even think of moving forward.

Step 8 – Make sure the CRM works per the Need Statement and SalesMap™ before you implement it with the sales team.

Step 9 – Train, train, train. Be open to influence from the sales professionals. Make mid-course modifications only after you confirm the changes work for the sales professional.

Step 10 – Revisit Step 1 monthly. Put it in your CRM as a recurring entry. Martha Stewart would be proud.

Expect efficiency to decrease with the use of CRM before it increases. With any new behavior, there is a loss of efficiency during the learning curve. Stick with it as efficiency will ultimately surpass the person system by a large factor.

Going back is NOT an option!!

Chapter 12
Impact 4: Best Practices, On-boarding, & Selection

Typically a manager would select the sales professional, proceed with On-boarding, and capture best practices as the process moves forward. For our purposes, this chapter goes in reverse order. It is helpful for us to begin at the end and work our way back as it is the best way to illustrate the key points.

Groundhog Day

In the classic movie *Groundhog Day*, Phil Connors, wakes up to relive the same day over and over and over. With each repeated day, Phil makes minor changes based on his mistakes and missteps from the previous day. Each day he sees the same people, relives the same scenario and navigates the same situation. At the end of the movie he incorporates all of his learning and executes the perfect day, winning everyone over including the love of his life. This would be a great model for the way sales organizations and sales professionals develop over time, except for a few key differences.

The characters, customers and scenarios in our sales story change frequently. Seldom are mistakes and missteps reviewed daily with modifications made for the next day. When we do figure out a best practice, seldom is it documented and then taught to the next generation of sales talent. At best it is a tribal story that gets lost within a month.

The methodology of how you capture the best practices, document the sales process and coach everyone up to speed will determine how quickly sales are generated. The unfortunate reality is that we rarely capture best practices and implement them across the team. We rarely document anything other than the operational processes of our company and yet, without a sale there is no need for operational excellence.

Revolving Doors and On-boarding

Your company will see an unprecedented addition of new sales professionals, sales managers and sales support team members on an increasing basis going forward. The waves of change reviewed at the beginning of this book will begin to feel like a sales tsunami.

Sales Leaders' On-boarding Challenge

As new talent arrives we bring them up to speed with on-boarding that is often operationally focused and similar to water-boarding. The other option may be the catch and release approach, letting them practice on customers. In some regards it is predictable because you, the sales leader, often are forced to ignore many of your management duties during the lengthy interviewing and hiring process. This may, if anything, get even worse. Once you have hired someone you need to get back to the work you had put on hold. Your options are to hand them off to the operations team, water-boarding, or unleash them on customers, catch and release. As the speed of the revolving door increases, you will have more spots to fill, and it will continue to become more difficult to find sales talent.

Attract and Retain

If we begin with what every sales professional wants in an organization, we can attract top talent and ensure their success. Success is the best retention tool. As you bring new sales professionals into your organization the key elements driving their success will be:

Leadership Support – The opportunity for the new sales professional to engage leadership in the sales process.

Network Access – As in your ability to allow the new sales professional to tap into the organization's network. At a minimum this includes the network of the leadership team, employees, associations the organization is involved with, and the industry groups your organization belongs to.

Robust CRM System – An effective and efficient sales system to support their sales process. This must include existing customer contacts so the new hire has a way to utilize referrals.

Sales Process Model – A clearly defined road map, call it a SalesMap™, incorporating the best practices for each step in the sales process. This will jump start their on-boarding as they take advantage of the best practices of existing and former sales professionals.

Support Tools – Including phone, tablet, computer, subscriptions for digital meeting tools, etc.

Sales Training Resources – You will pay for sales training whether you spend money for it or not. This should also include a Learning Management System (LMS) that incorporates the best practices of the top sales professionals.

Leadership Access/The Ear of Leadership – As they begin their tenure as a sales professional they must know they have both access to leadership and the ear of leadership.

Coaching – Sales coaching, account strategy coaching and self-improvement coaching both internally and externally.

Opportunities for Growth – My daughter was hired into a company right out of college. In her 12th month of work, she was approached by her district leader to discuss her next step with the organization. Within another year, the organization had relocated her. I remember commenting to a business associate how insightful this strategy was. With an average stay of 24 months, many employees would begin looking for new opportunities outside the company at 12-18 months. My daughter's company simply stayed ahead of that curve and kept a great employee engaged with future opportunities for growth within their organization versus outside their company. This is not different with your sales talent. Begin discussing different territories, account base and other opportunities within your company sooner rather than later.

Sales Professionals' On-boarding Challenge

The On-boarding process is a bit different for the sales professional. While it may seem after reading this paragraph like I'm being paid by sales managers to make this next recommendation, let me give you my reason for suggesting you stay at your current employer far longer than the current average.

In his book *Outliers,* Malcolm Gladwell[12] shares research showing a correlation between time invested in your job/passion and the attainment of success. The time invested relates to your time performing the essence of your job/passion. Gladwell's chapter 2, The 10,000 Hour Rule, suggests success seems to come after you have performed the essence of your job/passion in excess of 10,000 hours. It does not take long to realize this is going to be more than a couple of years. If you constantly change jobs the question is, will you ever achieve success?

---

[12] Outliers, The story of success, Malcolm Gladwell, copyright 2008 by Malcolm Gladwell, Published by Little, Brown and Company

So how do you decide which company to work for? When you make a commitment to become a sales professional in a referral-based world you need to choose your partner carefully. Part of a sales professional's evaluation of a potential employer should include the following:

Leadership Support – The availability and willingness of Leadership to actively participate alongside you in the sales process.

Network Access – The ability to tap into the network of everyone within the organization. Including leadership teams, employees, associations the organization is involved with and the industry groups the organization belongs to.

Robust CRM System – An effective and efficient sales system that supports and drives the sales process. This includes existing customer contacts so the new hire has a way to utilize referrals.

Sales Process Model – A clearly defined road map, call it a SalesMap™, incorporating the best practices for each step in the sales process. This will jump start your on-boarding and help you take advantage of the best practices of existing and former sales professionals.

Support Tools – This may include phone, tablet, computer, subscriptions for digital meeting tools, etc.

Sales Training Resources – A Learning Management System (LMS) that incorporates the best practices of the top sales professionals.

Leadership Access/The Ear of Leadership – As you begin your tenure you must have both access to leadership and the ear of leadership.

Coaching – Access to sales coaching, account strategy coaching and self-improvement coaching both internally and externally.

Opportunities for Growth – Lay out your plan of how you will meet the goals of both management and sales and your long-term aspirations for growth. Make sure leadership is on board from the start.

The first step for your success is up to you so pick the right organization to partner with, as you should be there for a long time.

Hire Right, from the Start

Now that you have a methodology for capturing best practices and providing the support and tools for successfully on-boarding new sales talent, you are down to the final element, selection.

"How do I know if they can sell?"

You know, or you should know. Behavior, motivation and values are predictable. You can assess a candidate's fit for the position you are hiring. Given the revolving door and the importance of finding the right sales professional, identifying the DNA of a great salesperson and other support team members for your company is essential to your long-term success. You cannot afford to miss. Given the trend toward a shorter stay at your company, you have to get results sooner from salespeople and that requires improved selection. Your ability to keep your funnel filled with potential candidates and compare them to your ideal candidate, will increase the probability of finding your next star.

Hiring a foolish person or anyone just passing by is like an archer shooting at just anything.
P.S. 26:10 (NCV)

Identify the bloodline of your top sales talent and stock your team with thoroughbreds. Once you find them, equip them with the tools, systems and information for them to be successful. Coach them for success. Capture their best practices along the way and feed it back into the system. As they succeed, give them greater opportunities. And repeat the process.

Chapter 13
Impact 5: Great Time for Great Companies and Great People

When you put each of the waves together you will begin to feel the cumulative impact:

- 10K/day of baby boomers retiring for decades to come. A seat is opened up and the surge of customers changing roles and organizations ensues.

- Higher frequency of career-hopping involving subsequent generations will add fuel to the fire. There will be more changing roles and more customers occupying new seats in new organizations as the wave continues to build.

- When a customer begins to ponder a purchase they head to the Internet long before they seek a conversation with a sales professional. If they find what they need on-line and the price is right they will never engage with a sales professional

- No one will hear or see sales prospecting calls as Unified Communications and big data predictive screening relegates them to spam.

- Committees and purchasing teams expand the number of contacts you need to cover

- Everyone is busier than ever before. Even if you do get through the labyrinth of technological barriers, people are not as inclined to take your appointment

However, all this combines to create great news for great companies and great people. The reason is simple. As contacts move around, and they will move around, they take with them the experience they had with you and your company. At the next stop, and the next stop, and the next stop, they will share the experience with others.

As committees expand, the new additions will talk with other stakeholders about the experience they had with your company. There is a good chance that someone you know, who has had experience with you, will know those stakeholders. We call this a referral-based world.

But there is one question that needs to be answered. How was the experience? If the experience with either you or your company was not great then prepare to hammer the phone and pound the pavement in hopes of finding a naïve prospect that is not aware of you or your company's reputation. The essence of sales success going forward will be how referable are you?

Long before the invention of the printing press, knowledge was shared verbally and the points were written by intellectuals. One such book of sayings, written nearly 3000 years ago and often referred to as wisdom literature, is Proverbs or the Mishlei.

These bits of insight were captured in very brief statements to encourage memorization. These wise sayings have stood the test of time and comprise the timeless wisdom shared in this book. Whenever you see a P.S. (Proverbial Saying) and the wise sage, we have included a direct quote from the wisdom literature.

Much like the P.S. in a letter, these wise sayings are the last thought we desired to share on a point being made. These wise sayings provide insight into how to become referable in a referral-based world.

> If you have to choose between a good reputation and great wealth, choose a good reputation.
> P.S. 14:21 (GNT)

Chapter 14
You Must be Good...to be Great

What is the key to becoming and remaining referable in a referral-based world? At the risk of oversimplifying the entire thesis of this book, it comes down to one primary point: You must be a good person. If you are a good person, then push on and you can become great! What makes a person good and then become great? That is the topic of the balance of this book.

Recently, I had the opportunity to make my first visit to the Grand Canyon. I drove an hour in the dark so I could be there to see the sun rise over and into the canyon. It was a beautiful day and the first word in my journal is Unbelievable! It was the only word I could think of to define the view as the sun began to rise.

After I took the typical tourist pictures, I walked around to a number of sites and came across the Kolb Studio.

Easy to miss from the road, the studio is perched on the side of the canyon. It was the home of the Kolb family since 1904, before becoming part of the Grand Canyon Association. The Kolb brothers were photographers and spent their life hiking and boating the Grand Canyon in search of amazing photographs and movies. As one of their movies played in the gallery it was clear their expeditions in the canyon were anything but safe or easy. In order to get their photographs and movies, they endured tremendous pain and overcame significant obstacles and setbacks as they traversed the canyon. It dawned on me this is no different for salespeople who want to become good on their way to great.

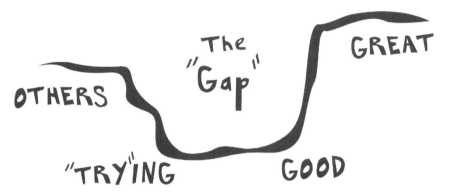

Looking at this illustration, one side of the gap is the mass of salespeople. Some, for whatever reason, will decide not to do the hard work necessary to learn the habits to be good and then great and will continue trying to be good salespeople.

In the gap are the salespeople who are becoming good through hard work and tremendous effort. They learn to overcome obstacles and setbacks. They keep their eyes on the target and continue moving forward despite the challenges.

On the other side of the gap are the salespeople who have endured pain, overcome obstacles and done the hard work in order to become good and finally great. These are the sales professionals who will be routinely referred. Where are you in this illustration? You should be aware, as your customers will tell you when you ask.

It is possible to slip back into the gap. However, the sales professional who continues to move forward to newer and higher levels, will put great distance between themselves and others in the gap.

To move from one side to the other involves timeless wisdom. Enjoy your journey from wherever you are to Good and ultimately to Great!

Chapter 15
Likability Leads to Good and Then to Great

Take one minute to think of the best person you have ever worked for. Write down words that define the reason that person was a good boss. In most, cases the words nice, good, friendly, or thoughtful will be on the list. For the purpose of this book, we use the term likability to define these traits. In order to be good, on your way to great, you must be likable.

It Shows so Shine

Likable shows. So you better rise to the occasion on every occasion. A few years ago we took our written Sales Octane values statement and created a Values Flag that consists of six separate colors. Each color represents one of our values[13]. One of the colors in the flag is yellow, which stands for, we strive to make a positive contribution to everyone, every day, in everything. It is a noble effort and it takes a lot of work, especially on challenging days!

A warm, smiling face reveals a joy-filled heart, but heartache crushes the spirit *and darkens the appearance*.
P.S. 15:13 (VOICE)

---

[13] Always give credit where credit is due. The inspiration for the values flag came from Matchstic, A Brand Identity House in Atlanta, Georgia. www.matchstic.com Thanks!

When You Give, You Receive

It starts with our face. Customers like you more when you smile than when you appear less than happy. Unless a person has spent significant time in the study of body language, most will not be able to discern a genuine vs. disingenuous smile. In the process of smiling, research shows you actually begin to create optimism in your own mind. Customers like you more and you feel better about your situation. It is a win-win.

Light in a messenger's eyes brings joy to the heart, and good news makes you feel better.
P.S. 15:30 (NIV)(GNT)

Over 55% of what your customer takes away from your conversation will be from what they see. So, help them see something good!

Your happiness will show in your eyes.
P.S. 15:30b (ICB)

Good or Bad, You Will be Known

You can only fake it so long. The good news is customers may not see it the first or second time, but the bad news is, it will eventually come out. The term is authenticity. Eventually the authentic you will be known. If you are a miserable person, eventually it will come through regardless of how hard you try to cover it up. This is good news for good people. So, be good on your way to great!

Every day is a terrible day for a miserable person, when he is cheerful, everything seems right!
P.S. 15:15a (GW)(TLB)

Treat others in a manner you yourself would want to be treated
- THE "GOLDEN RULE"

Golden Rule Point 1 – Ethics and Morals

The golden rule is a great place to start on your journey to become likable. The golden rule is wise advice involving ethics and morality. The sales professional is ethical and moral according to the standards of morality and ethics in the world they work. Sales professionals do what's right. Another color in our Values Flag is white. White stands for we do what's right. The sales professional should always do what's right.

> When you're kind to others, you help yourself;
> when you're cruel to others, you hurt yourself.
> P.S. 11:17 (MSG)

However the golden rule, when taken into the behavioral sciences realm, may cause us to lean into the punch so to speak.

Golden Rule Point 2 – It's About Them, Not You

The golden rule is essential, but it is only half the equation. As an example, take my behavioral style, Influencer/Driver, and put me into a selling situation where I am selling to someone with a behavioral style that is Compliant/Steady. If I "treat them in a manner I would like to be treated", as the golden rule states, I would lean into the punch. My behavioral style is not similar in any way to the behavioral style of the customer in this example. In order for the customer to like me, I will need to modify my approach to be similar to them. While this illustration is simple, the process is anything but.

> It's selfish and stupid
> to think only of yourself
> P.S. 18:1a (CEV)

In most cases, you call on multiple customers with multiple roles and as a result, multiple behavioral styles. Toss in the new reality of committees, and you now have multiple behavioral styles on the committee. As customers answer their phones less and communication moves to email, text, web meetings and the like, the sales professional must become a master of knowing how to adapt to their customer.

In *First 100 Days of Selling* and *First 100 Days of In-home Selling* we go in depth on the techniques to identify the behavioral style of your customer. We then explain exactly what to do so the customer will like you because they sense you are like them. The process involves four steps:

1. Know who <u>you</u> are. On the road to likability we need to know our strengths and our challenges. Once we know <u>our</u> style we need to...
2. Learn how to identify the customer's style. The sales professional needs to become a master at quickly discerning their customer's style. This takes practice. Once you know your customers style, we then...
3. Avoid denial. Some customers will naturally like you because they share similar behavioral style characteristics. Do not go into denial, other customers have a behavioral style that is nothing short of trouble if we don't follow step 4. The sales professional understands the reality of the fit and will...
4. Adapt. Every customer situation requires the sales professional to adapt, even if the customer is just like us.

In circumstances involving ethics and morality, follow the golden rule to a fault and you will become more likable.

In the behavioral science area, it is not about how you want to be treated, it is how the customer wants to be treated that matters. Remember It is not about you, it's about them. When we miss this distinction we go looking for trouble.

> Try hard to do right and you will win friends;
> go looking for trouble, and you will find it.
> P.S. 11:27(CEV)

Behave Yourself

You can control your behavior, but you can not control the consequences of that behavior. The good news is becoming more likable is totally in your control. The hard news is it will take effort depending on where you are in the GAP. But make no mistake, it is in your control.

Chapter 16
Honesty

Honesty is essential in a referral-based world. In order for your customer and others to refer you, they must trust you. Trust is like a bank account or what we will call the trust account. We make deposits into the trust account when we are honest and we make withdrawals from the trust account when we are dishonest.

Some deposits and withdrawals are small and others are large. Some withdrawals can even bankrupt our trust account. That happens when our referral stream dries up and we are left to find customers who are not aware of our reputation. In a referral-based world, if we work diligently to be honest, our reputation will precede us and work to our advantage.

House of Cards

If you stop to think about this; most of the time our dishonesty, even the little white lie, is driven by our perceived need to skew the truth in order to get what we want. We fear the truth will cost us the sale. In sales, it is typically telling the customer something we know will move them in the direction we want them to go, or avoid putting up a barrier to slow or derail the sale. Here is the problem: When the customer finds out we misled them, we bankrupt the trust account. No referrals, ever.

But back it down a bit. What if you get the sale and then there is an issue down the line. For example, we tell the customer they will have delivery in seven days even though we know it won't happen. They place the order based on our seven-day lead time. Eight days later we are frantically trying to explain the situation. Even if they don't ever figure out we misled them, we still lose. Do you think they will refer you? It's a house of cards.

Dishonest gain will never last, so why take the risk?
P.S. 21:6 (TLB)

Honesty Impacts more than Just You

Sales has become a team sport. In most cases you have various team members that support you: customer service, project management, installation and a host of others. When you make it a habit to manipulate the truth, deceive customers or outright lie, your team knows. Their trust in you diminishes.

Without the trust of your team, your performance will suffer and you end up in a position where you need to manipulate even more to cover your tracks. You are only hurting yourself. You will never have a healthy relationship with your team or customers when you practice dishonesty.

So how does the sales professional build trust through honesty. It starts at the top.

Honesty Starts at the Top

Ask any leader what qualities they look for in their team and trust will be at the top of the list. The minute trust erodes relationships begin to falter. Leaders who cultivate an environment of honesty develop a culture of trust. It is no different with sales professionals.

Think of yourself as the leader of ME, Inc., because once you enter sales you truly are self-employed! So what do you want to cultivate in your company? As you cultivate honesty you make consistent deposits into the trust account with your customers. Customers love sales professionals who are honest!

 Good leaders cultivate honest speech
P.S. 16:13a (MSG)

In the Sales Octane Values Flag the color blue stands for our value we do what we say we will do as in true blue! It is a nice way of saying we strive to be honest and trustworthy. Oddly enough, our customers seem to appreciate our honesty even when it is not what they want to hear! Truth equals trust and truth is a deposit into the trust account.

 Leaders love advisors who tell them the truth.
P.S. 16:13b (MSG)

Honesty Starts Small

We have all heard the concept behind the little white lie. No one will notice. It is just a small withdrawal so it won't be an issue, right? It is a slippery slope.

First we make our habits, then our habits make us.
– Charles C. Noble

Honesty is a habit and habits begin very, very small. If you ever tried to lose weight or break any bad habit, you know how hard it can be. But think about how simple it was to start the habit. More often than not, you do not remember how the habit even started. Every bad habit begins slowly and without a lot of effort. Before long it becomes part of who we are. On the other hand, every good habit begins slowly and takes a lot of effort. Before long, with consistent and persistent effort it becomes part of who we are. Begin with a zero tolerance approach!

 <u>Never</u> talk deceptively don't <u>ever</u> say things that are not true
P.S. 4:24b (ISV) (EXB)

Honesty Always Wins

Start making deposits into the trust account today regardless of their size. If you are consistently moving in the right direction with this important habit, when you slip, and you will, you will bounce back quickly and get back on track. Those who ignore this wise counsel will eventually get caught in their own trap and the fall is great! Your customers and your team will know your level of trust. You will be known.

Good people might fall again and again, but they always get up.
 But those who are evil trip and fall when trouble comes.
P.S. 24:16(ERV) (NIRV)

Authenticity – It's Not an Act, It's at the Core

At the very core of this time-honored principle is the issue of authenticity. You can only pretend to be honest for so long before the house of cards will fall. Honesty needs to be at your core the same way a gyroscope navigates a plane.

Honesty will keep you on the right path. Honesty will create trust with your team and your customer. Honesty will always win more often in a referral-based world than deceit and dishonesty. Start practicing the habit of honesty today!

The wisdom of a sensible person guides his way of life but the folly of fools is deception.
P.S. 14:8 (NOG)(NIV)

Chapter 17
Patience

Selling is a game of confidence. When you are confident, it shows. When you believe in your solution because you have seen it make a difference for your customers, it shows. If your primary interest is what works best for the customer, it shows.

Conversely, if you are under pressure it shows. Desperation reeks of pressure. When you need the sale it is almost as if you telegraph the pressure you are feeling to the customer. You see their concern and confidence erodes even more.

What does the wise sales professional do? They practice patient persistence.

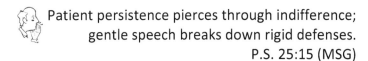
Patient persistence pierces through indifference; gentle speech breaks down rigid defenses.
P.S. 25:15 (MSG)

The term patient persistence sounds like an oxymoron, two conflicting words like jumbo shrimp. Let's separate the two words and illustrate how the combination is very powerful for the sales professional.

Patience Versus Frustration

Patience, in the context of sales, is nothing more than avoiding the semblance of irritation or frustration. When I telegraph my frustration or irritation at any point during the sales process, the customer becomes uncomfortable and typically moves away.

When I telegraph patience, it comes across as a level of confidence. Confidence in my solution, confidence in my company, and confidence in my ability to help the customer with their situation. Not arrogance but humble confidence. Patience is a form of persuasion or influence leveraging humble confidence.

Persistence Versus Pushy

There is a fine line between being pushy and demonstrating persistence. The wise sales professional knows how to stay on the side of persistence without crossing over to pushy. We call it staying in form and it takes a lot of practice.

- Persistence is asking great questions to uncover the need or the source of the customers' concern.
- Persistence is taking responsibility by assuming control of the next step.
- Persistence is following up consistently to reinforce accountability.
- Persistence is following through on what was promised.
- Persistence is a bias toward being proactive!

Persistence becomes pushy when:

- You find yourself constantly telling the customer about your product or service with little or no interest in the customer's situation, problem or need.
- You find yourself showing frustration and irritation when the customer doesn't "get it."
- You leave appointments with the customer in control of the next step.
- You haphazardly call the customer when it fits into your schedule in a failed attempt to following up.

These actions send the message you are only interested in their order, not their satisfaction with your solution.

Fast is the Enemy of Patience and Persistence

If you need it fast you will almost always telegraph impatience to the customer. Slow and steady always wins the race and is the path of the wise sales professional. Long term is what matters in a referral-based world.

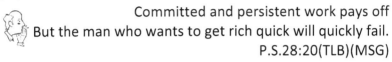
>Committed and persistent work pays off
>But the man who wants to get rich quick will quickly fail.
>P.S.28:20(TLB)(MSG)

Fear is the Enemy of Patience and Persistence

In their book *What You Fear Is Who You Are,* Dr. David Thompson and Krysten Thompson illustrate how our most inappropriate behavior, including behavior that drives good people *and customers* away from us, is often driven by fear.[14]

The sales professional is motivated to win. This is good! The motivation may come from their desire for the customer to experience the benefits of their product because they know their product is the best (Compliant Behavioral Style).

The motivation may come from a desire to get results both for them and for the customer (Driven Behavioral Style).

The motivation may come from a desire to help the customer (Steady Behavioral Style).

The motivation may come from a desire to please the customer (Influencer Behavioral Style).

---

[14] What You Fear Is Who You Are, David Thompson, Ph.D. and Krysten Thompson, published by MTR Corp, 2000, emphasis mine

All of these motivations are good. It is when we fear we are not accomplishing whatever is motivating us, we become impatient and pushy with the customer. The answer? Stay in form.

Stay in Form – The Disease of Dis-ease

The word "disease" might as well be hyphenated "dis-ease" when it comes to the sales profession. When we become uneasy (dis-ease) with the direction the sales call is taking it typically results in the disease of frustration. For some salespeople the symptom of the disease is talking too much (Influencer). For others it's aggression (Driven). On the other side of the table are the salespeople who pull back and shut down (Steady) or become defensive (Compliant). Staying in form requires the sales professional to know what motivates them and understand the situations where they are most likely to fall out of form. Once you know those scenarios you can develop your go-to routine and stay in form.

Driven/Driver – Pull back!

Patience is better than strength.
Self-control better than political power.
P.S. 16:32(ICB) (MSG)

Influencer – Stop talking!

Whoever restrains his words has knowledge,
and he who has a cool spirit is a person of understanding.
P.S. 17:27 (ESVUK)

Compliant – Let it go. It's not about being right!

 Sensible people control their temper;
they earn respect by overlooking wrongs.
P.S. 19:11 (NLT)

Steady – Keep asking!

 Patience leads to abundant understanding,
but impatience leads to stupid mistakes.
P.S. 14:29 (CEB)

It's Not About Being Right; It's About Getting What You Want

I am sure you can think of a time that you have misunderstood a situation. It is human nature. Your customer is no different from you. In an appointment, you may be doing a great job of sharing your capabilities and diagnosing their situation but they see it differently. This creates a situation, where the sales professional must stay in form, not react, but rather patiently evaluate the situation and look for a different approach.

In some cases the indifference you feel from the customer or the outright defensive stand they are taking is just who they are. Don't take it personally. Skeptical or Dogmatic may be their behavioral style! Properly diagnosing the behavioral style of your customer will help you in these situations. Stay patient and in form as you look for another way to approach the challenge.

The key is not to allow their indifference or defensive position to transfer to you. When you become stronger or forceful in a situation, you are actually transferring the power to the other side of the table. If you want to have influence and power with your customer, start with patience and control. Do not force it with your power.

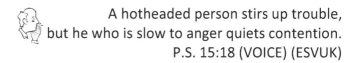 A hotheaded person stirs up trouble, but he who is slow to anger quiets contention.
P.S. 15:18 (VOICE) (ESVUK)

Slow and steady

Pull back, stop talking, let it go and then keep asking! One sales technique we share with our customers is the, "I'm OK!" approach. If you've used it, you know how counterintuitive this technique felt, or even sounded, the first time you used it. However, the process of not forcing the situation but rather pulling back creates a similar transfer of power and pulls the customer back towards you.

In the seconds and minutes following the transfer of power the sales professional will think of additional questions and strategies to patiently persist!

Practice Patience

You have heard the statement, practice makes perfect. I propose this is not true. Practice makes permanent. Case in point, golf.

Golf is an interesting game. In the northern states springtime is greeted with great enthusiasm by amateur golfers. Heading off to the driving range with their newly acquired weapons, they purchase a large bucket of range balls. With little or no warm up, planning or preparation, they begin to hit the range balls toward the green abyss. Sliced, hooked, bladed, topped, skulled and shanked is a normal result. By the time the last ball is hit they are only marginally improved, and in most cases, the hook or slice is now permanent. Practice makes permanent.

As a friend of mine once said when I asked them for advice about my golf swing, "amateurs teach amateurs to be amateurs." Ouch. In order for an amateur golfer to improve their game they must get lessons from a professional and then practice. Practicing without wise counsel is only going to marginally improve your game.

In order to become patiently persistent, the sales professional must get wise counsel in their development and then they must practice the routines to help them stay in form. Perfect practice makes perfect and permanent.

Chapter 18
Humility

The Humble Sales Professional. Those words may not seem like they go together, however, research is clear. Humility is an essential characteristic of the sales professional who wants to be seen as a leader in their field. Right off the bat we have the issue with the word itself. It seems like a sign of weakness. A few years ago I came across a definition for humility that I think fits the purposes of this application. It is from the book, *Humilitas*, by John Dickson. In short, humility is NOT the absence of power. Dickson defines humility as "the noble choice to forgo your status, deploy your resources or use your influence for the good of others before yourself".[15] Think about those three characteristics:

1. Noble choice to forgo your *status* for the good of others before yourself;
2. Noble choice to *deploy your resources* for the good of others before yourself; and
3. Noble choice to *use your influence* for the good of others before yourself.

It is all about others before yourself. What happens when we don't take this position?

Pride Comes Before the Fall

We have all heard the statement and it is packed with timeless wisdom. Think about this: When we are prideful, we feel as if we know it all. So how does one get better when they know it all? The sales professional has been taught they need learn the customer's situation, identify the customer's need, and uncover the value the customer will experience with the solution. These

---

[15] Humilitas by John Dickson, pg. 28, copyright 2011 Zondervan Publishing

three words; learn, identify, and uncover, require us to open up our minds to the customer's situation and be open to new information. If we are not willing to learn, we will just show up and regurgitate our product or service information to them. What happens when we show up and regurgitate vs. learn?

> Pride precedes a disaster,
> and an arrogant attitude precedes a fall.
> P.S. 16:18 (GW)

Humility Leads to Improvement

How can we improve if we are not willing to admit we don't know everything? We can always get better! The sales professional views every situation as an opportunity to learn from others including the customer. They are open to influence and have a mindset of, I am here to learn vs. I am here to spew. This demonstrates that the sales professional is humble and willing to learn in the mind of the customer.

> Fools will be punished for their proud words,
> but the words of the wise will protect them.
> P.S. 14:3 (NCV)

Humility Leads to Wisdom

When we approach situations with humility, being open to the fact we do not know everything and can always get better, we begin to move toward being wise in the mind of our customer. Wisdom seems like an academic term but it is quite simple. Wisdom involves a combination of knowledge, experience and sound judgment. As you gain more knowledge and experience you become wiser. As you make good decisions you become wiser. This is why humility is so critical. When we are prideful, we don't think we need knowledge. When we are closed to new knowledge, we close ourselves to new experiences. And when we lack knowledge and experience, we can not make good decisions with sound judgment.

> When pride comes, disgrace follows,
> but with humility comes wisdom.
> P.S. 11:2 (HCSB)

Humility Leads to Honor

As we open ourselves to influence and improvement through increased knowledge, experience and sound judgment it comes back around in the form of honor. We have all witnessed examples of individuals, who, when receiving an award; humble themselves before the audience. We incorrectly assume that once we become honored we will also assume a posture of humility. This rarely is the case. Honor does not precede humility. It is the other way around, humility precedes honor.

> Before a man's downfall, his mind is arrogant,
> but humility precedes honor.
> P.S. 18:12 (ISV)

Clearly, we want our customer to see us as wise and sing our capabilities to others in the form of referrals. This will happen if we get the above-mentioned steps in the proper order. Humility leads to knowledge and improvement, It opens us up to experience and helps us make sound decisions. Then, and only then, will we be seen as wise and our reputation is paid forward in a referral-based world.

One more step in the process. Who should sing our praises?

Leave the Singing to Others

The last three words of John Dickson's' definition of humility says it all, "others before yourself." The key to growing in humility is to do the work in service to others, and let them sing your praise and tell others about your capabilities.

 Don't call attention to yourself; let others do that for you.
P.S. 27:2 (MSG)

 One of the keys in securing referrals and having your customers share their positive experience with others is to ask for referrals. There are only two reasons you are not getting referrals: 1) you don't deserve them or 2) you are not asking. The sales professional deserves referrals so we can eliminate the first hurdle. For the sales professional it all comes down to asking. In a referral-based world you must get your customers to refer you, and while organic referrals are great, we want to do everything possible to get the process moving.

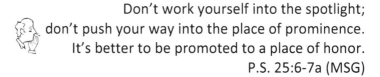 Don't work yourself into the spotlight; don't push your way into the place of prominence. It's better to be promoted to a place of honor.
P.S. 25:6-7a (MSG)

Don't push! Ask. In the *First 100 Days of Selling* series, we go into detail about how to ask for referrals; it is a lot of work. When our daughters were young, we would take them to a playground near our home. The playground had been there for years and there was a very, very old merry-go-round. It took a lot of effort to get the merry-go-round turning. But once I got it moving, I would only have to occasionally give it a passing nudge to keep it going.

The referral stream works the same way. It takes a lot of effort up front to get it moving, but once you put the referral system in place, it begins to fuel itself. Your responsibility and effort turns to putting new customers into the system and occasionally giving the rest of the system a nudge. In a referral-based world, your customer's voice will cut through all the noise from your competitors and deliver your message for you to your next customer.

One Last Test of Humility

As you practice humility the referrals and praise will begin. Others will recognize your contribution and you will be known. But know, this is a test.

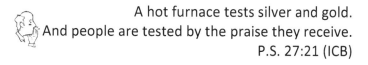

A hot furnace tests silver and gold.
And people are tested by the praise they receive.
P.S. 27:21 (ICB)

When this happens and the accolades and the praise arrive, revisit the definition of humility. Make the noble choice to "forgo your status for the good of others before yourself." Shift the compliment to others who helped you and you will not get burned. Keep the focus off of you

> If you have foolishly been proud or presumptuous—put your hand on your mouth
> P.S. 30:32 (NABRE)

Replace with Generosity

There is a logical order to all this. Pride precedes disaster, disgrace and downfall. Humility precedes protection, wisdom and honor. Pride leads to negative referrals, and humility leads to positive referrals. So how do you learn the new habit of humility? Simply keep the focus off of you and turn it towards others. As we take the focus off us and move it to others, we begin to practice humility, replacing pride with generosity. And generosity is another avenue in our journey of moving from good to great.

Leaders: It Starts at the Top

If you are in a leadership position, take note. Pride is like a cancer spreading throughout the organization. It is often not noticeable until it is too late. Humility starts at the top. You are in a position where you too must place "the good of others before yourself." Hire others of the same mindset and your organization will flourish.

> Get rid of a conceited person, and then there will be no more arguments, quarreling, or name-calling.
> P.S. 22:10 (GNT)

Chapter 19
Generosity

The remedy to pride "is not attempting to think of yourself less but to think of others more".[16] If we constantly beat ourselves up for our arrogance and pride we will do just that, beat ourselves up. This is unlikely to produce change. It is hard to beat someone into improvement. However, if we begin to focus more on others, customers in this case, we have less time to focus on ourselves. The best way to practice humility is to practice generosity. It's like getting two for the price of one.

Many people see themselves as being generous. Taking customers out for meals, sporting events, handing out tickets and holiday gifts are among the items mentioned whenever I ask sales professionals the question, "how are you generous towards your customers?" These gifts of generosity are fine, but not totally adequate. We need to broaden our definition of generosity to include words, resources, talents and time.

Generous with Words

One of my favorite training venues is in the wine country of Northern California. Across the street from our usual venue is a marvelous drive-in called Taylor's Refresher. The word refresher brings a lot of good things to mind. The generous sales professional refreshes others with their words. Look for opportunities to positively reinforce those around you and watch how the reinforcement returns.

A generous person will prosper; whoever refreshes others will be refreshed.
P.S. 11:25 (NIV)

---

[16] *Satisfied*, Jeff Manion, copyright 2013, Zondervan Publishing

Do you want to prosper? Then be a refresher with generous words. Take the focus off yourself and turn it towards your customer.

Generous with Resources

When you hear resources you could think money. Think well beyond money. Your customers have needs beyond the product and service you provide. In the L.I.N.K. process, the "N" in the acronym stands for Needs. Think of your network of resources as a means to help your customers. Needs could include a connection you know within your network to help your customer. Needs could include an article you read, that might be of personal interest to a customer. Sharing your resources includes both personal and professional. The sales professional has immense resources because of their vast network. Be generous with your resources and you move the focus from your needs to the needs of your customer.

Generous with Talents

Sales professionals have a very broad range of talent. Social skills, people skills, listening skills, problem solving skills and networking skills are at the core of the sales professional. As you earn the trust of your customers, they will open up their life to you in a way where you can be generous with your unique abilities.

Do not hold back anything good from those who are entitled to it when you have the power to do so.
P.S. 3:27 (NOG)

Listen and look for opportunities to help in any way you can with your immense talent. By focusing on ways to help your customers with your talent, you move the focus away from yourself.

Generous with Time

Customers will want you more urgently as time moves forward. Just in time, 24/7/365, connectedness, and customers waiting longer in the buying process to engage with you, will result in higher expectations around Response Time. The sales professional must become a master at time management so they can be generous with their time when the customer wants to engage.

> Lazy people will cause their own destruction because they refuse to work.
> P.S. 21:25 (ERV)

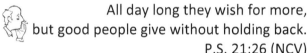
> All day long they wish for more, but good people give without holding back.
> P.S. 21:26 (NCV)

Generosity Requires Doing Something With Action

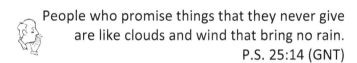
> People who promise things that they never give are like clouds and wind that bring no rain.
> P.S. 25:14 (GNT)

If you have ever been in a situation where you need rain, you can relate to this analogy. Maybe it is a burned up lawn or a backyard garden and you are on the verge of despair, then you see the storm clouds roll in. There is hope, as you see the promise of rain. Then the winds begin to blow and the storm seems certain. You sit on the front porch peering toward the skies. But slowly the winds subside, the clouds disappear, and you realize the promise of rain was just "wind" and "empty" clouds.

When we make a promise to reward someone and fail to follow through, we are just like the empty clouds and wind. When we fail to reward someone who gives us a referral, it is even more devastating because a precedent is being set. The referrer realizes that you do not follow through on your promises and stops sending you referrals. Psychology Of Selling Principle #6 states, "Whatever you reinforce you get more of." This is critical when it comes to following through. You did not follow through. The referrer is reinforced that you do not follow through, therefore, you get what you reinforced, no more referrals. Become a person of your word and give those rewards and watch how your situation improves.

Generosity is Hard Work

At the very least, you will feel better about having helped another with your words, resources, talents and time. In many cases, your customer will respond with their appreciation, which further reinforces your generosity. And, in some cases your generosity will help open doors to other connections.

 A gift opens the way for access to important people.
P.S. 18:16 (CEB)

One of the benefits of a referral-based world is the way in which your generosity will be known to others, including leaders. News travels, good or bad. In the case of the generous sales professional, it travels fast.

The Boomerang Effect

In many ways generosity is counterintuitive. How can you give and actually receive more in return? A good friend of mine shared with me an interesting comparison. Imagine holding a stick and a boomerang. Both are wood. Both can be thrown. One comes back, and one does not. Greedy salespeople look at generosity as if it were a stick. When they throw a stick to a customer, it does not come back and therefore, they have less. The obvious conclusion is don't give and you'll keep what you have. The sales professional looks at generosity as a boomerang. When they are generous toward others most often the generosity returns even more.

 Some people give freely and gain more; others refuse to give and end up with less.
P.S. 11:24 (ERV)

 When you give you will receive. Looking for, or expecting, the return on your investment is not the reason you give, however, the principle still exists. When you give, you make an investment in someone else and in most cases you will get a return! At the very least you will increase your generosity, which moves you closer to good and then on to great.

Give freely, and you will profit. Help others, and you will gain more for yourself.
P.S. 11:25 (ERV)

Chapter 20
Self-Control

Another requirement in being referable in a referral-based world is self-control.

When our daughters were growing up we had a tradition of reading a bedtime story. They all had their favorite books and so did Jane and I. My favorite was *If You Give a Moose a Muffin*, by Laura Joffe Numberoff. This well-written and masterfully illustrated children's book tells a story of a Moose who arrives on the doorstep of a young boy's home where he is immediately offered a muffin to eat. Instead of consuming the muffin, the moose needs jam and as he heads off to get the jam he is distracted. The book is one comical distraction after another. The moose is pulled in twelve different directions until finally, at the end of the story, the muffin is consumed. We could easily change the moose to a salesperson and the muffin to a contact/lead/prospect (the shiny objects being chased), and the distractions suffered by the moose would pale in comparison to the number of distractions faced by a sales person.

Self-Control Defined

The concept of self-control seems punitive or constraining. For the sales professional it is imperative to stay in form. Years ago I was introduced to this phrase, stay in form, by an attorney who shared with me how they coached their clients. Stay in form was code for thinking before responding. Stay in form was code for not reacting spontaneously. Stay in form was code for using pre-determined responses. Stay in form was code for not allowing emotion to get in the way of a good decision. Stay in form is the key for the sales professional to remain cool, calm, focused and move from good to great.

The prudent see danger and take refuge but the simple keep going and pay a penalty.
P.S. 27:12 (NIV)

Self-Control for the Future

The term "prudent" gets a bad rap. It reeks of the root word prude, which certainly does not define the vast majority of those in the sales profession. However, prudent simply means, "acting with or showing care or thought for the future." Prudence means making decisions that are in the best interest of your future vs. the moment. When we stay in form we think of our future.

Self-Control with Focus

To be clear, I struggle with focus and my guess is some of you deal with the same challenge. For the last several years I have tried numerous techniques and approaches to reign in my desire to pursue bright shiny objects. To reinforce the realities of all the distractions I face in a week, I kept my electronic notepad with me and kept a list of the distractions. Here is a partial list:

- Call comes in as I am about ready to make a call.
- Do I have the wrong phone number?
- Open up CRM to get a phone number and the password needs to be changed.
- My computer Operating System needs to be updated.

- The program/app needs to be updated.
- I can't find the password for a program.
- My printer is not connected, WiFi issue.
- I have to download firmware for printer.
- A customer needs a copy, I can't find it, I have to create a new document.
- I look for an email I know I sent and during the process of looking for the email I noticed another urgent item I was supposed to respond to.
- I could not find a document but found another file I was looking for which led me down another path.
- While at a social media site doing some quick research I noticed someone I knew who was looking for a position.
- My password needs to be changed per security requirements.
- My WiFi is down.
- I need to upgrade programs.

Staying in form with all the interruptions and distractions takes a lot of self-control. Our innate desire to please others causes us to exchange our future for the moment. Every time we chase after the next shiny object we exchange our future for the moment. It is a poor trade-off. However, as discussed in the earlier chapter on Generosity, the sales professional needs to be generous with their time. Here's the rub. In order to make this work efficiently and effectively we have to make sure we are working with qualified customers.

 Those who waste their time on worthless projects are foolish.
P.S. 12:11b (ERV)

It's helpful and interesting to evaluate your distractions. Try keeping a pad of paper, your day-planner or your electronic note pad handy and keep track of all the interruptions that come your way during the week. Call those worthless projects. When we get to the chapter on Organization and Planning your Work you will need this data.

Self-Control with Interruptions

As you head down the path of self-control the first step is to think before you act.

 Wise people always think before they do anything.
P.S. 13:16 (ERV)

Your brain works faster than you mouth. Before agreeing to something use a few nano-seconds of brain time to determine if this is the best use of your time. A few seconds of silence feels like an eternity to the salesperson. In reality it is a second or two and the customer will never notice. When you say yes to something you say no to something else. This is a principle of life. When you say yes to the interruption you say no to the higher priority activity you were engaged in. So, when you say no to the interruption you are saying yes to your future.

Self-Control when Conflicts Arise

There are numerous situations where the customer may disagree with the salesperson. I have listed four in the order of escalation:

1. Customer politely disagrees with a particular point.
2. Customer does a dis-service to the salesperson (inconsiderate).
3. Customer strongly objects/disagrees.
4. Customer argues with the salesperson.

The sales professional understands the long-term view and stays in form regardless of the disagreement.

People who refuse to argue deserve respect.
Any fool can start an argument.
P.S. 20:3 (ERV)

Think first, then ask questions. If you are prone to argue when things don't go your way, then you need to figure out a new routine. When things are going our way we tend to be at our best. Under moderate pressure we tend to come across differently than when we do under extreme stress. The sales professional knows how they react under pressure and develops their go-to response. It's called adapted behavior and sales professionals who know just what they will do and how they will respond in an escalating situation know how to defuse the confrontation.

 A person with a bad temper stirs up conflict.
But a person who is patient calms things down.
P.S. 15:18 (NIRV)

Slow Down

Once again, patience comes to the rescue. Don't react, or worse, over-react. Instead slow down and think. If you run into a similar situation more than once it is best to write down the situation, and get some counsel from others on how they would have handled the situation. Figure out your new routine, practice it and then the next time you will find it easier to stay in form.

You may be Right

Everyone loves to hear they are right. One option when confronted is to offer a subtle encouragement to the customer such as, "you may be right," and then pause to ask a question. You diffuse the situation with your positive statement and it buys you time to identify your question. The key is to stay in form and trust the fact your brain works faster than your mouth. Buy yourself time to think rather than react!

 It is to one's honor to avoid strife, but every fool is quick to quarrel.
P.S. 20:3 (NIV)

Help Me Understand

Another approach is to probe deeper by suggesting you need their insight to understand their position. This simple request for insight, "help me understand," puts the customer back in a position where they will have to talk and share more information. This buys you time to listen and figure out your next strategy.

How so?

Another option to diffuse the situation and buy yourself more time to gather your thoughts is to simply ask the question, "How so?" If you have raised children, you know how maddening it is when they continue to ask why? If you listen to yourself or observe another parent during this incessant routine you will notice the parent will typically add information every time the child asks "Why?"

Parent: It's time to go to bed
Child: Why?
Parent: Because it's 8 o'clock and that's your bedtime
Child: Why do I have to go to bed at 8?
Parent: Because that's when you go to bed, otherwise you'll complain tomorrow when I wake you up! Now get upstairs!
Child: Why do I have to go to bed and she doesn't
Parent: you are younger, your sister went to bed at the same time when she was your age!
Child: Why, I'm not tired?

But here's the question, why do we feel we need to constantly provide additional clarification? It is human nature. When you ask the question, "How so?" the customer will elaborate on their position, and while they are talking, you are listening. Remember, you have plenty of brain time to figure out your next approach as long as you *stay in form*.

A fool gives full vent to his anger
but a wise man keeps himself under control.
P.S. 29:11 (WEB)

Drop it

Occasionally, the best response is simply to drop it.

Starting a quarrel is like breaching a dam;
so drop the matter before a dispute breaks out.
P.S. 17:14 (NIVUK)

It is not about being right; it is about getting what you want. Keep the long-term goal in mind. Oftentimes, the absolute best technique is to avoid engaging. Stay in form, get out, get wise counsel and come back to challenge when you have a proactive strategy.

Self-Control with Success

As you begin to move from good to great and your referral stream grows you will win more business. It is important for the sales professional to stay in form whenever you are rewarded with business or whenever someone congratulates you on a win. Be humble. Say a genuine, "thank you," and shift the focus to others, including your team and the customer, be generous.

Don't be happy when your enemy is defeated;
don't be glad when he is overwhelmed.
P.S. 24:17 (NCV)

Self-Control with Words

 Wisdom is found on the lips of the discerning,
but a rod is for the back of one who has no sense.
P.S. 10:13 (HCSB)

Discernment and good judgment go hand in hand. Knowing when to talk and what to say is a critical part of staying in form as you move from good to great.

Chapter 21
Speech

Bringing value to your customer is not only limited to the features, benefits or advantages they receive with the use of your product or service. Bringing value includes every facet of what you bring to your customer. And speech, what you say and how you say it, is critical.

In order to become the trustworthy sales professional and take advantage of a referral-based world, the sales professional must choose the right speech.

Be Positive

As a speaker on the topic of selling I meet a lot of new people at sales conventions. Often someone will approach me and say, "Hey do you happen to know someone by the name of. . .". Their next statement goes one of two ways. They either say something good or they say something negative, judgmental or share a bit of gossip about the person.

I have noticed over the years my reaction is to pair the individual standing in front of me with the comments they are making. If they say something good about the mutual acquaintance, I see them as good. If they say something negative, cynical or a bit of gossip, I see them as being negative, cynical, or a gossip. Everyone loses. The person being spoken about loses, the person in front of me loses, and I loose since there is nothing positive coming out of the conversation.

Pair yourself with a positive and you become positive to those around you. The same way you need water when you are thirsty, everyone you talk to needs something positive.

Like cold water to a weary soul
is good news from a distant land.
P.S. 25:25 (NIV)

Anxiety weighs down the heart,
but a kind word cheers it up.
P.S. 12:25 (NIV)

It is foolish to speak scornfully of others.
If you are smart, you will keep quiet.
P.S. 11:12 (GNT)

Build Up as You Head Up

As decisions involve more stakeholders, you will likely head up the ladder within the customer's organization. The higher you get in an organization the greater the probability you will engage with managers. When you are discussing team members with their manager REMEMBER the old adage if you don't have anything good to say, don't say anything at all.

Never slander a worker to the employer,
or the person will curse you, and you will pay for it.
P.S. 30:10 (NLT)

Less is Best

The best strategy is often to say less. This may be a significant challenge based on your behavioral style but all styles will benefit from simply saying less. Because the brain works faster than the mouth there is a natural tendency to want to say what is on our minds. As Mark Twain once said, "It is better to keep your mouth closed and let people think you are a fool than to open it and remove all doubt."

 So avoid people who talk too much.
P.S. 20:19b (ICB)

Keeping a Confidence

The sales professional is often like a traffic director at the crossroads of both their own organization and the customer's organization. When information is shared in confidence, there is an opportunity to use that information to increase ones self-worth. This is nothing more than violating a confidence or gossiping. Both make us feel wise because we know something that others don't know. We may gossip to position ourselves as better than the person we are gossiping about.

We have all been told something with the lead in, "Can you keep a secret," or "You didn't hear this from me," and then were told information that was either given to them in confidence or was nothing more than gossip. How did you feel? In most cases you quickly conclude if you are telling me another person's secret, then you are probably also telling other people my secrets. At that point, trust is eroded.

Because your network will become your net worth we need to have the confidence of everyone. The sales professional keeps a confidence so their customers can have confidence in them.

 A gossip goes around revealing secrets, but a trustworthy person keeps a confidence.
P.S. 11:13 (CJB)

 And a person who gossips ruins friendships.
P.S. 16:28b (ICB)

Competition

Ask yourself, if the information you are sharing is true. Honesty is a pivotal ingredient in being referable so dishonest or misleading information is out of the question. But what if you have a Feature, Benefit or Advantage (F/B/A) over your competition, is that a good reason to negative sell? The best technique is not to tell a customer what a competitor's product or service won't do. This is negative selling and it will pair you with a negative. The best approach is to tell the customer what your product or service does, a positive, and finish with a question:

- How is the competitor approaching that F/B/A?
- What is the competitor able to do?
- Use an assumptive statement that raises a F/B/A of your product or service by assuming your competition offers the same F/B/A. For example: "now when our competition (insert your F/B/A) how does that work?"

In each case you have honestly shared your F/B/A and raised the issue with your customer. In many cases you arrive at the same point where the customer understands the shortcoming or disadvantage of your competitor's product and you have remained positive in the process.

 Don't give evidence against others without good reason, or say misleading things about them.
P.S. 24:28 (GNT)

Clean – You Can NOT Lose

There are two options with regard to your speech: Clean and Less than Clean. Depending on your choice of language you stand to win or lose points with your customer. While there are significant variations between the type of unclean language and the level to which you can win or lose points, it is undeniable there is a greater probability of winning with clean and losing with less than clean.

Quadrants

Let's take a moment and look closely at these four quadrants and how they may relate to winning or losing a sale.

	YOU WIN	YOU LOSE
CLEAN	**2** Possibly — *"I like that Salesperson; they didn't swear"*	**1** Never — *"That Salesperson didn't swear; I don't like them"*
LESS THAN CLEAN	**4** Never — *"That Salesperson swore a lot; let's go with them!"*	**3** Possibly — *"I was uncomfortable with that Salesperson's language; I'd rather not work with them"*

Quadrant 3

Looking at quadrant 3, let's say you use less than clean language and your customer is a person who uses clean language. Do you believe the customer has ever thought, "That salesperson swears a lot. I'm uncomfortable with them"? Possibly? Probably? On the other side, if you use clean language, how often have you said to yourself, "that salesperson swears a lot. I'm uncomfortable with them"? My guess is you are answering absolutely. And you can possibly think of some recent situations where this has occurred. One can conclude you may possibly LOSE points with your customer depending on your customer's view point or standards. Is it possible to WIN with less than clean language?

Quadrant 4

So, with less than clean language you can possibly lose, but you will never win. Looking at quadrant 4, let's say the salesperson, uses less than clean language. When was the last time you believe a customer who uses clean language has said, "They swear a lot, lets go with them"? Never! You LOSE. But even if both you and your customer use less than clean language, do you believe it is the primary reason they like you? Frankly, because you are both acting in a similar manner they probably don't think about it. If they like you in that situation, it is not because of your language.

 One whose tongue is perverse falls into trouble.
P.S. 17:20b (NIV)

Quadrant 1

Now lets look at the dynamics of using clean language. Regardless of whether you use clean or less than clean language, think of a time when you met with a salesperson who was using clean language. Did you think to yourself, "That salesperson is not swearing, I don't like them"? If you are being honest, you never thought about it, not once. Clean language is neutral. If a salesperson uses clean language, they can NEVER lose.

Quadrant 2

But can you actually WIN points with clean language? Let's say you are a salesperson who aspires to consistently use clean language. If your customer also uses clean language how often do you believe they have said, "That salesperson does not swear, I like them for that"? Possibly. So, the salesperson may win some points for likability. However, if you are a person who uses less than clean language, have you ever said, "That salesperson does not swear, I like them for that"? Possibly, but most likely the answer is "no, but I do remember noticing they were not swearing and I thought that was odd." Odd does not usually result in dislike. So, we are NOT saying you WILL win, but you may possibly win.

Final Scenario

If your competitor comes in with less than clean language and you come in with clean language, and the customer aspires to use clean language, you WIN with clean language and in a big way because of the differentiation.

Bottom line is you can NOT win with less than clean language but you can NOT lose with clean language. Why not take the path where you cannot lose?

If They do it, Shouldn't I?

A good friend of mine and fellow trainer shared with me they have heard their clients say, "If the customer swears first, then it's ok for you to swear." On the surface it may seem logical as it lines up with our Psychology Of Selling Principle #2, People buy from people like themselves. However, what if the customer just slipped because of the situation? What if their slip was totally out of character? I have slipped many times. If you assume you have a green light for a stream of expletives you LOSE.

It's what you don't see that can hurt you. The customer may, in fact, be very comfortable with less than clean language, but what about their spouse, significant other, literally anyone within hearing. Worse, what if those within hearing represent a referral?

Years ago I heard a counselor talk with a group of teenagers about this same issue. Before sharing the topic he began with an illustration. Handing a new tube of toothpaste to one of the kids along with a paper plate, the counselor told them to squeeze out as much of the toothpaste as possible onto the plate with a single squeeze. In an effort to prove their ability in front of the group this kid wrapped their hand across the entire surface and squeezed with all their might. A large heaping pile of toothpaste emerged from the tube to the plate. Elated at their conquest they extended the plate toward the counselor. The counselor did not take it but instead gave the next instruction, "Now get it back into the tube."

Like the toothpaste, once it's out, it's out. You cannot WIN with less than clean and you cannot LOSE with clean. Begin to create the habit of clean and watch the referral stream grow.

Chapter 22
Listen

This entire project, Selling by the Book Today, began with a single observation. After being in business eight years, and running close to 1,000 sales professionals through our sales assessment, we discovered over 60% of them shared one characteristic, they loved to talk. This was right about the time when I came across this piece of timeless wisdom, a chattering fool comes to ruin, and I thought that's pretty strong.

 but a chattering fool comes to ruin.
P.S. 10:8a (NIV)

Then, less than 15 seconds later, I saw it repeated, again.

 and a chattering fool comes to ruin.
P.S. 10:10a (NIV)

Only five times in the entire book, where there are over 915 proverbial sayings, it was the first time the author had repeated himself for emphasis. I thought this must be important or the author would not have mentioned it twice. Even more alarming in both cases the counsel concluded with the same statement of what would happen to the chattering fool, they would come to ruin. Clearly the person who translated the material into English chose "ruin" to reinforce the point. However, when I went back to the original word and the original meaning it was worse. It basically means, you are done, finished or ruined. Not for the day, not for the situation, but forever. That was the day I decided to begin this project.

The context of these two occurrences involves accepting insight and instruction, and trustworthiness versus deception.

The wise in heart accept commands,
but a chattering fool comes to ruin.
P.S. 10:8a (NIV)

 Whoever winks maliciously causes grief,
and a chattering fool comes to ruin.
P.S. 10:10a (NIV)

 The two are connected. When we are not open to the insight and instruction from our prospect we tend to chatter more. When we attempt to deceive our prospect we tend to chatter more. On the other hand, when we chatter less we become trustworthier, and gain insight and instruction from our prospect. Trust and insight is a powerful combination.

In researching the behavioral style results of the sales professional, it is clear the vast majority of those in the selling profession are born with the gift of chatter. It's in their DNA. Since so much of the sales process involves speaking with customers this is a great gift, some would say essential. But every strength has a corresponding challenge. It's like a double-edged sword.

 Have you met a person who is quick to answer?
There is more hope for a fool than for him.
P.S. 29:20 (GW)

If you like to talk, you run the risk of talking too much. When we talk too much we become the chattering fool. In order to be good or trustworthy and move from good to great we need to talk less and listen more.

Denial is Not Just a River in Egypt

Through the use of a profiling tool we discovered well over 60% of those sales people tested have the trait of being extroverted, people oriented/cooperative or a combination of both. Both characteristics are a catalyst for having our string pulled. Think of the character Woody in the Toy Story series. He is enthusiastic, optimistic, social, people oriented and whenever someone pulled his string he was sure to talk. One must understand your own behavioral style and learn the techniques to adapt your natural style to situations where you want your prospect to share. The stronger your extroversion and people orientation traits the greater the need for adapting your behavior. This is a direct hit for me given the fact my extroversion and people orientation is 100%. For me, it literally could not get any worse. I am the original chattering fool, however, I'm not in denial.

Selling is not telling. You don't learn much of anything when you are talking or telling about your solution. Other than what you can see, the only way you learn is from what a customer tells you. If you are on the phone, you can not see anything so the only time you learn is when the customer is talking. Therefore, the more we solicit input, insight and instruction the more we learn. The more we learn the more tailored our response and we are gaining trust along the way.

 Wise people are quiet and learn new things, but fools talk and bring trouble on themselves.
P.S. 10:14 (ERV)

A PROBLEM WELL STATED IS A PROBLEM HALF-SOLVED.
- Charles Kettering

The better you define the problem the better you are positioned to figure out how you are going to address the customer's problem with the value of your product or your service.

Talk Less = Increased Value

A common refrain from salespeople is everyone is buying on price. A wise friend, Alan Gottardt, author of *The Eternity Portfolio*, shared with me an interesting insight, "Price is only an issue when your value is in question."

The issue is always price if we have not created value in the mind of the customer. When we don't create value the only point of differentiation becomes price, and that is often a losing battle. If the sales professional is going to increase the value of their solution, they must get the customer to share their challenges. The customer will not be able to share if the salesperson is doing all the talking. By talking less and getting the customer to talk more you dramatically increase the probability of identifying a problem and this positions you to build value. It is the only way to stay out of the price war.

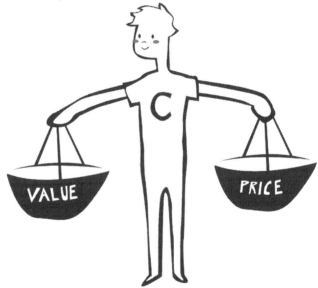

Talk Less = Reduced Suspicion

> It's stupid and embarrassing to give an answer before you listen.
> P.S. 18:13 (CEV)

Somewhere around 1990 the refrain, wait for it, became the catchphrase to build suspense when sharing news. It is also a great place to start when overcoming the chattering fool syndrome.

When we resolve an issue too fast we cause suspicion. If you wait longer to share your solution, there is a greater chance you will uncover additional problems with the customer's current situation and increase the value of your solution.

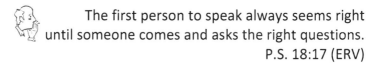
> The first person to speak always seems right until someone comes and asks the right questions.
> P.S. 18:17 (ERV)

It is human nature to want to provide an answer quickly in order to get the customer to like us. However, in many cases this will actually minimize the impact of our solution. The customer may feel like they have been searching and struggling with the issue for some time and wow, you show up and in minutes you can solve the problem. The salesperson is thinking, "They are going to love me when they hear this." To the customer this feels as if, "I just shared a problem I've had for some time and you come in here telling me it is a simple fix. Now I feel like a fool because I didn't think of the solution before".

> Anyone who answers without listening is foolish and confused.
> P.S. 18:13 (NCV)

Just because you have the knowledge, does not mean you should share it right away. If your sales process involves more than one conversation, then it is far better to take the information back to your team to get alternative views.

> A fool finds no pleasure in understanding
> but delights in airing his own opinions.
> P.S. 18:2 (NIVUK)

We always think we have all the answers. The reality is we have all the answers that *we can think of.* And those thoughts are entirely the result of our knowledge and our experiences. When we engage others to get alternate views of the situation, we gain their knowledge and their experiences, both of which typically add great wisdom to our final solution.

> Listening to good advice is worth much more
> than jewelry made of gold.
> P.S. 25:12 (CEV)

Talk Less = Empathy

Empathy is an essential trait for the sales professional. One characteristic of empathetic sales professionals is their ability to put themselves in the shoes of their customer.

> Wise people want to learn more,
> so they listen closely to gain knowledge.
> P.S. 18:15 (ERV)

Empathy requires suspending judgment. It requires taking a real interest is what the customer is sharing. And most importantly, it requires the sales professional not to assume their solution can help the customer as they approach a situation. First, they must understand the customer's situation. That will determine how, or even if, there is a fit. And they must be willing to walk away and not prescribe their solution if it does not fit the customer's diagnosis.

 The prudent keep their knowledge to themselves
P.S. 12:23a (NIVUK)

Talk Less = Avoid Sales Malpractice

When you hear the word diagnose, it is typically in the context of medicine. We go to the doctor with an issue and are asked a lot of questions. The doctor will not prescribe anything until they are confident they have accurately assessed the situation. What are they worried about? Easy, a malpractice lawsuit. What if salespeople could be sued for sales malpractice?

 Do not go out hastily to argue *your case*;
You will be embarrassed if someone else proves you wrong.
P.S. 25:8 (ERV)(NASB)

Do not be too hasty to get to your presentation. Do not be quick to tell about your solution. Make certain you have properly diagnosed the customer's issue by qualifying the opportunity and accurately assessing the situation before you begin sharing your solution.

 The one who listens will speak successfully.
P.S. 21:28b (HCSB)

It's just math, talking less equals fewer mistakes. The more you talk the greater the statistical probability you will say something you wished later you would have kept to yourself.

 You will say the wrong thing if you talk too much—
so be sensible and watch what you say.
P.S. 10:19 (CEV)

The math could work to your advantage. If the customer is doing more of the talking, the probability increases that they will share something they may wish later they had not shared. It could be something about their budget, the poor performance of their current provider, the name of another decision maker, or even the fact they really are planning to move forward with you regardless of your price.

 Watching what you say can save you a lot of trouble.
P.S. 21:23 (CEV)

We have all heard the quote from Abraham Lincoln, "Better to remain silent and be thought a fool than to speak out and remove all doubt." Oddly enough, Lincoln did not come up with this idea. An avid reader himself, Lincoln repurposed the statement, captured two thousand years prior in the Proverbial Sayings. Pretty wise of him.

We think even foolish people are wise if they keep silent. We think they understand what is right if they control their tongues.
P.S. 17:28 (NIRV)

Talk Less = Humble

Earlier we talked about the importance of humility. Talking less actually increases your humility in the eyes of others. The salesperson is often overly optimistic and talks as if they already know they will win the sale only to lose it. As a result of their optImism, combined with their fear of rejection, the sales person misdiagnoses the reality of the situation and fails to cover the bases. They take their foot off the gas and hope they can coast across the finish line and win the sale. They take the position with others in their company that they are all set and do not need input. They are closed to others' insight and are not willing to go down any additional paths because in their mind they have it all wrapped up. They speak in haste, counting the sale before it is won.

 Do you see someone who speaks in haste? There is more hope for a fool than for them.
P.S. 29:20 (NIVUK)

Just to be clear, when we talk less we:
- Learn more
- Increase value
- Reduce suspicion
- Show empathy
- Avoid sales malpractice or misdiagnosis
- Increase our knowledge
- Have fewer mistakes
- Be humble

How do we talk less? It's simple, ask better questions. It sounds easy in theory, but requires significant effort.

> Getting information from someone can be like getting water from a deep well. If you are smart, you will draw it out.
> P.S. 20:5 (ERV)

Customers are often reticent to share everything with a salesperson until they begin to feel the salesperson is trustworthy. Trust incorporates likability and competence. If you look through the bullet points above you will find each result will increase trust.

The sales professional develops their questions early on in the development of their sales approach. During the process they gain wise counsel from others, including customers, whose insight and knowledge is essential. They practice the questions and modify the questions based on response. With every new product, service or market dynamic they go through the entire process again to add, delete or enhance their questions. The sales professional should never engage with a customer without having their questions in front of them, or have proven their ability to remember the questions to perfection.

Sales professionals never practice on their customers. They develop their questions and practice with their team. Once the sales professional knows the questions, they will be very good in front of a customer and on their way to being great. And great gets referred often in a referral-based world.

Chapter 23
Knowledge

Customers are more knowledgeable than ever before. There is more information available a web-browser and click away than ever before. Your customers wait longer in the buying cycle to engage with a salesperson, and most customers have already obtained knowledge about your services. New customers want to know if you are relevant.

Knowledge Makes You Relevant

A lot is said about being relevant in our noisy world. How do you stand out? Some say be crazy, loud and different. However, customers see through the smoke of bright shiny objects and ultimately will look for something of true value.

rel·e·vant
CLOSELY CONNECTED OR APPROPRIATE TO THE MATTER AT HAND

In the world of the sales professional, the matter at hand is the customer's business, situation, needs and challenges. And, since you are reading this book, it is fair to suggest you are trying to become a top sales professional. As a result, let's eliminate the "or" in the definition and go for both closely connected and appropriate! So, to be relevant we need to be *closely connected and appropriate to* the customer's business, situation, needs and challenges. How does one become closely connected and appropriate?

Have you ever passionately and enthusiastically headed down a road only to discover you were headed in the wrong direction? It could have been while driving somewhere or possibly a sales strategy. You were positive you were on the right path and were going to win the sale only to find out you missed something along the way. Passion and enthusiasm can often lead us in a direction only to find out later it was the wrong direction.

 Being excited about something is not enough. You must also know what you are doing.
P.S. 19:2 (ERV)

For over two thousand years, the Proverbial Sayings (P.S.) referenced throughout this book, have been referred to as Wisdom Literature. The World English Dictionary defines wisdom as, "the ability or result of an ability to think and act utilizing knowledge, experience, understanding, common sense and insight."

When you combine knowledge with passion something amazing happens. Typically, customers pick up on your passion for your product/service and that gets you in the door. Once you are in the door you will find the customer already has so much information they are looking to you for additional knowledge.

Knowledge Magnet

There is no shortage of knowledge available to those of you reading this material. Whether you are holding this book in your hand, or reading this on your tablet, or your smartphone or even listening to the audio version, you will agree that knowledge is available 24/7/365. But who and where you get your knowledge from, and even how, is critical.

Once you begin to pursue knowledge, you become drawn to the people, resources and interests that help you become more relevant. We have all heard the statement readers are leaders. Leaders in the sales profession are just that, leaders. With books on tape, e-reader options and the rise of mobile and tablet solutions, it is interesting that in 2014, over 50% of the American population read or listened to less than five books over the course of the year.[17] What are the other 50% doing? Hopefully they are working for your competitor.

The Sales Octane Values Flag includes the color green for our value, we embrace learning. Green is the color of growth. With all the forms of information out there the sales professional needs to throw themselves into gaining knowledge in their area of expertise.

The mind of a person with understanding gets knowledge.
P.S. 18:15a (EXB)

Knowledge Pursued

Knowledge is not something you simply absorb through the years of selling your product. Much of the knowledge will come from other sales professionals and leaders both inside and outside your organization, other thought leaders. We must pursue knowledge and not simply hope it pursues us.

A discerning mind seeks knowledge,
but the mouth of fools feeds on foolishness.
P.S. 15:14 (HCSB)

The sales professional needs to spend more time with others who are pursuing the same level of sales and industry excellence. Every minute you are with others who possess wisdom you must be willing to learn. Since my schedule includes close to 100 days a year at annual sales meetings, I get to see how salespeople

---

[17] Pew Research Center, January, 2014, "E-Reading Rises as Device Ownership Jumps"

interact with each other. Do they feed on each other's knowledge or feed on trash? What are you feeding your mind?

 A wise person is hungry for knowledge, while the fool feeds on trash.
P.S. 15:14 (NLT)

Every encounter is a learning situation and an opportunity for you to increase your knowledge. The key is to listen and learn.

 Intelligent people are always ready to learn. Their ears are open for knowledge.
P.S. 18:15 (NLT)

Notice the wisdom comes when we engage our ears and keep them open for knowledge. You have to choose to be ready to learn.

Knowledge Test

Listen to the top performers. The old statement, misery loves company is true. When salespeople are underperforming, one natural avenue is to share their negative knowledge with anyone who will listen, especially a new salesperson. Test the source of the knowledge being shared.

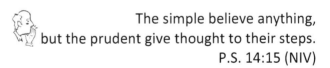 The simple believe anything, but the prudent give thought to their steps.
P.S. 14:15 (NIV)

Top sales professionals are often very humble. They have confidence in their ability and their proven track record, but they are always more than willing to help others. They also use their time wisely. When you meet with top sales performers make certain you come prepared with a clear set of objectives. Share your challenges and your long-term goals for self-improvement. When the top performer sees your sincerity, they become the essence of our definition of humility by forgoing their status and deploying their resources and influence for your good.

 Those who make fun of wisdom look for it and do not find it,
But knowledge comes easily to someone with discernment.
P.S. 14:6 (NCV)(CJB)

Years ago I heard a speaker who shared a cute riddle. He said whenever we have a challenge we have a choice. The choice is to become bitter or better. I have never forgotten this insight. In sales, it is inevitable we will lose along the way. Rarely will we have a Groundhog Day experience where we can consistently have a do-over day after day after day with no long-term impact.

A fool who repeats his foolishness is like a dog that goes back to what it has thrown up.
P.S. 26:11 (NCV)

The question is, how will we deal with the loss? By evaluating our losses and asking for wise counsel on alternative options, the mistakes will make us better. The alternative, choosing to be bitter, will pretty much insure we will make the same mistake again. Make mistakes count by engaging others in a post-mortem, whether it's a win or a loss. Leverage and capture your best practices when you win and identify alternative strategies when you lose. Otherwise you will be one sick dog.

There are many cute quotes about becoming an overnight success in 10, 15, 20 years. The point is always the same. There **is** no overnight success. The tendency is to look at the one-in-a-million situation where someone absolutely hit it out of the park in a short period of time. Those situations are one in a million. The good news is your competition is getting discouraged after a year or two and they jump to another overnight success opportunity.

The sales professional knows it will take time to become respected in their space. In a referral-based world it will take less time as long as you are good while you become great. Back to the merry-go-round. A lot of work, but it works.

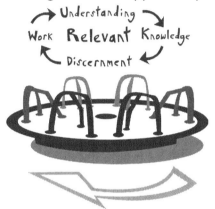

Starts at the Top, Again

 wise and knowledgeable leaders bring stability.
P.S. 28:2b (NLT)

Wise and knowledgeable leaders embrace the pursuit of wisdom and knowledge. It is what brought them to their respected position and they strive to continue learning. The wise sales professional aligns with leaders who are willing to provide access to knowledge and wise counsel. This is how you go from good to great and get to the other side of the gap.

Chapter 24
Connections

Once you become referable how do you put that strength to work? One area is expanding and leveraging your connections. Without connections you will either need to be incredibly lucky or start off incredibly wealthy.

The rich have many friends;
the poor have none.
P.S. 19:4 (CEV)

"Once I'm successful then I'll have time to work on my network." This is a common refrain with new and even seasoned salespeople. It's sort of like the chicken and egg conversation, what comes first?

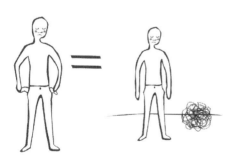

It is common to see those with wealth surrounded by many friends. Wealth is like a magnet. But what came first, the wealth or the friends? Hollywood aside, it's not the wealth. When you look around at top earning sales professionals, they earned their wealth the hard way. Starting at the bottom they worked hard to develop their network of contacts and customers. They were good people doing great work so their customers spoke well of them. They became highly referable. And moving forward in a referral-based world, they will be greatly rewarded. So what came first, the wealth or the friends?

Quality or Quantity

You may remember a car commercial in 2011 featuring a young adult with her 687 social network friends and her concern that her parents only had 19 friends. It was a great commercial meant to reinforce the fun the parents were having over the daughter "living" in front of cyber-friends on social media. While we laughed at the tongue-in-cheek commercial, in a referral-based world both are necessary. Moving forward, the sales professional must look at networking and connections in two dimensions: Deep and Wide.

Deep and Wide

There is no better picture to illustrate the actions the sales professional must take to grow their connections than a tree. Some trees have a root system that goes incredibly deep and others a root system that grows incredibly wide. The sales professional must have both.

The Guinness Book of World Records lists the deepest root depth is the wild fig tree found in South Africa. It's roots are in excess of 400 feet deep. The arid climate requires the roots to penetrate deep into the rocky soil. In the same way the sales professional must extend deep into existing and prospective customers alike.

As the revolving door spins with existing customers, the sales professional must have deeper relationships than ever before. No one wants to get the call telling them their customer contact is no longer with the company only to realize they have little connections beyond that person.

 Riches can disappear fast.
And the king's crown doesn't stay in his family forever
so watch your business interests closely.
P.S. 27:23-24a (TLB)

To go deeper the sales professional is always working up, down and all-around their customer's organization. Identifying and engaging with the levels above, below and on par with your contact will never get better than while your contact is still there.

 Good people are like trees with deep roots.
PS 12:12b (CEV)

So, are you good? A customer's willingness to share names and provide introductions is a direct reflection of whether they find you referable.

During your regular account reviews with your customer ask who would likely take over should they be promoted? This is a positive reinforcement in their direction and may surface additional contacts for you to engage on a deeper level. Develop your target list of titles and roles you wish to meet and arrive at every appointment prepared to deepen your network.

It is no different with prospective customers. As committees become more prevalent, it is essential the sales professional get as deep into the organization as possible. Account strategy sessions need to include a list of the titles and roles you will aim to identify as you begin the sales process.

Even if your sales process is business to consumer, this principle will apply to your business partners, suppliers and circles of influence. So, go deep with your connections. Remember, the deeper the root structure the more difficult it is to take out the tree.

But it is not enough to go a mile deep with our customers. The massive amount of customer movement going forward means you have the opportunity to grow your sales with every transition. The sales professional with a wide base of connections will be positioned to leverage the changes in a referral-based world.

Standing in front of a massive Redwood tree towering 200 or more feet into the air and a diameter of 20 feet you might be surprised to learn their roots are relatively shallow. The depth of the roots for a typical Redwood tree is only 4-6 feet deep. How does something so large and tall survive an average 500-700 years with such a shallow root structure?

The answer is in the way the roots tie together with other Redwood trees as far as 100 feet away. Weaving their network of roots together the Redwood trees support each other and allow each other to feed off their area. This is a great analogy for the power of going wide with your network.

The sales professional understands they must have an expansive network to take advantage of all the changes happening in the industry. With each change will come opportunity to grow their business as long as they have someone they know who is willing to refer them. Knowing when a customer changes organizations and where they are going will be a given for the connected sales professional. In most cases, you will be notified automatically when the change takes place. Having someone to refer you will depend on the width and depth of your network.

When the question is asked, "are you inch deep, mile wide or mile wide, Inch deep?" The answer needs to be, "mile deep, mile wide!"

 Take care of a tree, and you will eat its fruit.
P.S. 27:18b (CEV)

How do you "take care of the tree?" While this is a moving target, several over-riding strategies are key as you go deep and wide with connections.

Grow Your Social Media Connections

For the sales professional the seven degrees of separation must be zero or at the most, one degree of separation. If customers are willing to refer you, and you are widely networked, you cannot lose at securing an introduction.

The challenge is always time and knowledge. There seems to never be enough time to put a system in place and we will never have all the knowledge of options available and which is best. But we must figure it out or we will miss the opportunity to leverage the referral-based world.

Spontaneity needs to be planned and every contact should become a connection. This will only happen when you ask and take control of the process. Prior to every planned conversation, you need to know whether you are connected with that person. If you are connected, see below under "Search." If you are not connected, take the initiative to get connected.

Every unplanned or spontaneous conversation with someone you meet, take the initiative to get connected. Have your process down long before you walk into the networking venue. The opportunity to commit a new acquaintance to accepting you into their social network will never get better than those spontaneous conversations.

After the meeting, you must follow through. The sales professional must circle back around and invite the contact into their social network.

IT'S NEVER CROWDED ALONG THE "EXTRA MILE"
– Fortune Cookie

Respond immediately to changes in status – It is possible you will be getting announcements on the job changes in your network everyday. Respond immediately while your lazy competitors let it set. The potential opportunity is right in front of you. Establish an efficient process for how to quickly respond to those daily updates.

 Lazy people bury their hand in the bowl; they won't even put it to their mouth.
P.S. 19:24 (CEB)

Search – Pre-call research and Pre-call/appointment plans must include a review of the contacts you will be meeting and who they know. This may mean a referral name you can mention, or in some cases, it will be a target customer they may know. You never get a second chance so take advantage of every meeting whether over the phone, web or face to face. Utilize the full capabilities of the search and research the tools available.

Put your marketing drip campaign in place – Allow the marketing resources of your company to help keep your name in front of connections. Once your marketing department sees the effort you put into developing a wide network of accurate information, you have earned the right to request relevant information to share with the social network. It starts with you.

Align your Customer Relationship Management (CRM) system with your social media connections – Most CRM systems have the ability to access your social media connections directly from the CRM system. This will make your pre-call research and planning more effective and efficient.

Circles of influence – This is like hyper-growth fertilizer for your networking tree. Go deep with those connections who work in the same industry and markets with non-competing products or services. While this takes time to develop, their network becomes your network as the transfer of trust takes place.

Engage everyone in your organization – The system must involve everyone in your organization as you tap into social media and set the net. Every employee, regardless of their role, engages with contacts outside your company. As the employees expand their own network, the sales professional can tap into the array of networks and get even wider.

Never give up on a competitively held account – Go deep and wide over a long period of time and you can unseat even the most entrenched competitor. Sooner or later your competition will make a mistake. Sooner or later someone who will refer you will enter their organization. Sooner or later the person blocking you at the competitively held account will leave as a result of a job change or retirement. Go deep and wide, be patient and persistent and you will have your chance.

Bring value to your connections – Take a look back at the chapter on generosity. There are now more cost effective and efficient ways to bring relevant information and value to your connections than ever before. Bring value.

Set the net – The social "net"work you establish will:

- catch the positive referral when they leave an organization;
- the positive referral when they arrive at an organization;
- the negative detractor when they leave an organization; and
- the negative detractor when they arrive at an organization.

All four situations are a win for you. Including the last situation because you can immediately build your base of supporters to minimize their negative impact on others.

Over time the landscape for how to engage with your connections will change. As these changes occur we will continue to post relevant information about how best to take advantage of those changes. It is a moving target, so get moving.

In his book *41 A Portrait Of My Father*, George W. Bush shared, "While connections can open doors, they cannot guarantee success."[18] This is so true. If you have connections but you are

---

[18] 41, A Portrait Of My Father, by George W. Bush, copyright 2014 by George W. Bush, Published by Crown Publishers, page 41

not good then the connection will not lead to success. However, without connections the door will be shut. With connections the door will be open and the referable sales professional, who is moving from good to great, will achieve success.

Chapter 25
Wise Counsel

Top performers in every athletic discipline get coaching. We expect athletes to have coaches, but for whatever reason, most salespeople have not. There are so many benefits to putting a system in place in order to gain wise counsel.

Avoid mistakes – There are only two ways to get experience:

- jump in and get the experience first-hand (school of hard knocks); or
- find someone who has experience and learn from them.

The second option is a lot faster and less painful than option one. We incorrectly assume the only way to get experience in life is first hand. When we make a mistake we chalk it up to experience and avoid the mistake in the future. However, if we gain wise counsel from others it is possible to avoid the mistake right from the beginning.

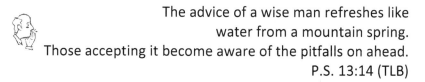

> The advice of a wise man refreshes like water from a mountain spring. Those accepting it become aware of the pitfalls on ahead.
> P.S. 13:14 (TLB)

Leverage their learning – You only learn from what you have experienced in your life unless you leverage others who may have additional experience. One significant benefit of obtaining wise counsel is to speed up your development as a sales professional. No matter where you are in your development, there is always more to learn.

Teach a wise man, and he will become even wiser.
Teach a good man, and he will learn even more.
P.S. 9:9 (ICB)

Increased humility – Humility is a necessary characteristic of sales professionals. The arrogant know-it-all is the antithesis of humility. You won't know what you don't know until you expose yourself to wise counsel. Once you start the process you will grow in knowledge and humility.

 Any bragger you correct will only hate you.
P.S. 9:8a (CEV)

As iron sharpens iron so people can improve each other.
P.S. 27:17 (EXB)

Increased following within your organization – When others see your willingness to improve in knowledge and humility through wise counsel, they will desire the same result.

 Walk with wise people and become wise;
befriend fools and get in trouble.
P.S. 13:20 (CEB)

Grow your counsel outside your organization – Wise people hang around with other wise people. Engaging with others in the pursuit of wise counsel leads to others sharing their resources to further your development. These connections will help in the future.

 Listen to advice and accept instruction,
that you may gain wisdom in the future.
P.S. 19:20 (ESV)

Improve your probability of success – Because customers engage salespeople later in the buying process, and have already gained knowledge before they reach out to you, the sales professional has one chance. With wise counsel we can approach every customer's unique situation correctly right from the start.

> Without counsel plans fail, but with many advisers they succeed.
> P.S. 15:22 (ESVUK)

Where should this counsel come from – This should come from as many different points of view as possible. Counsel can come from anywhere and anyone. The more counsel, the more wisdom.

> Where no counsel is, the people fall: but in the multitude of counselors there is safety.
> P.S. 11:14 (KJV)

Leadership, customers, other sales professionals, industry leaders, thought leaders, the list is endless. One group often left off the list are those prospects who choose to go in another direction. We don't like the poor customer evaluation any more than we like losing a sale. However, there is tremendous value in understanding why we lost the sale or failed to meet their expectations. Add the lost prospects to your list of people to engage for wise counsel.

How do you select wise counsel – Find those who are wise themselves. This may seem obvious, however, you want to receive wise counsel from those who frequently engage in the process of being coached and counseled. Would you use a coach who does not value their own self-improvement?

> With pride comes only contention,
> but with the well-advised is wisdom.
> P.S. 13:10 (KJ21)(NET)

Find those who are sincere in their willingness to help. What is motivating the wise person to provide insight and counsel? If they are sincere about helping, then you have found a good resource. But if the person providing the counsel is only interested in promoting themselves, you will want to weigh their insight carefully. This is the main reason to expand your coaching group beyond the people you work for and with. Their self-interest will often cloud some of their counsel.

> The heartfelt counsel of a friend
> is as pleasant as perfume.
> P.S. 27:9 (NLT) (TLB)

Align yourself with those of good legal, moral & ethical standing. Whomever you surround yourself with, you will become. If you pursue counsel from individuals who have a poor legal, moral or ethical track record, there is a good chance that is the type of counsel you will receive.

> Don't envy evil people,
> Have no desire to be around them.
> P.S. 24:1(CEB) (ERV)

> A good man's mind is filled with honest thoughts;
> an evil man's mind is crammed with lies.
> P.S. 12:5 (TLB)

Pursue reliable, dependable, wise counsel. Eventually you will rely heavily on wise counsel especially in seasons of significant need. If the counsel proves to be reliable and dependable during the easy times, it will be there when you need it the most.

Trusting an unreliable person in a difficult time
is like a rotten tooth or a faltering foot.
P.S. 25:19 (HCSB)

Align yourself with those who are willing to share what you need to hear versus just sharing what you want to hear. Wise counsel does not place their popularity with you above the greater good for your improvement.

 A refusal to correct is a refusal to love;
but whoever loves him is diligent to correct him.
P.S. 13:24 (MSG)(ISV)

The goal of gaining wise counsel is to leverage the wisdom of another. Surround yourself with wise people and you become wise.

 Stay away from a foolish man,
for you will not find competent advice
P.S. 14:7b (ISV)

Surround yourself with fools and you become a fool. In the long run foolish people seldom succeed in sales. The counsel you receive from fools will only harm your long-term development.

 A fool trying to say something wise is
Like a thorn-bush in a drunkard's hand
P.S. 26:9 (ERV) (NIVUK)

Wisdom and wise counsel is often incorrectly associated with age. The sales professional receives wise counsel from both young and old. My father, at age 92, has a great deal of wisdom, which I seek out and honor on a regular basis. However, when dealing with issues of technology, I not only need to gain wise counsel from someone much younger than him but also much younger than me. The wisdom literature used in this book was written to an agrarian culture. There was no electronic technology, no corporations and very few soft skills. So wisdom came primarily with age and life experience.

> We admire the strength of youth and respect the gray hair of age.
> P.S. 20:29 (GNT)

The sales professional will pursue wise counsel from someone who has recent experience. Oftentimes we seek counsel from someone who has done it before but their experience is from many years ago. The most beneficial input will be from those who have recently dealt with the very issue we are contemplating. In his book, *Stumbling On Happiness*[19], Daniel Gilbert shares how our minds play tricks on us. Over time our memories of experiences fade from back in the day and we unknowingly provide untimely wisdom. The sales professional gains wise counsel from those whose experience is most recent.

When to engage with wise counsel – Wise counsel will be beneficial when the sales professional is planning or strategizing. This may include account strategy, territory strategy, personal development strategy and team strategy to name just a few. Planning may include annual plans, long term plans and even daily/weekly/monthly and quarterly planning.

> Get advice if you want your plans to work don't go charging into battle without a plan.
> P.S. 20:18 (EXB) (GNT)

---

[19] Stumbling on Happiness, copyright 2007 by Daniel Gilbert, Published by Alfred A. Knopf

When confronted with a difficult challenge, albeit customer, career or personal, the first stop for the sales professional is their network of wise counsel.

A friend is always loyal,
they are there to help when trouble comes.
P.S. 17:17 (NLT) (NIRV)

But be warned: After you have received correction, it is essential to get additional insight. Too often the sales professional sees themselves as an island between customers, leadership and their own team. Having another unbiased sounding board is essential.

The road to life is a disciplined life;
ignore correction and you're lost for good.
P.S. 10:17 (MSG)

Listen to their counsel – A few years back I was engaged by a corporation to coach a salesperson who was having a difficult time. The timeless wisdom, fools think they know what is best, defines exactly the way I felt every time I talked with this person about what changes would improve the poor results he was having. Even though I was sharing proven principles, this person had a different take on the issue. After several unsuccessful attempts, I suggested to leadership we not continue our coaching discussions. The sales person and I would remain friends but I could not continue to offer coaching without implementation. Months later this person was let go.

Fools think they know what is best,
but a sensible person listens to advice.
P.S. 12:15(CEV)

Years later, I ran into him after he had experienced a number of difficult failed events. He asked me the question, "What do you think it is Jim? Why do you think things don't work out for me?" I shared the essence of the two challenges I believed were in the way of positive results in his life. While he did not disagree, he simply shook his head "OK," and went away without addressing the issue. It has been years now and this person continues to fall far short of his capabilities. A tragic result for a talented individual.

As a sales professional, you need to surround yourself with wise counsel and accept the coaching. Here are some steps I use when receiving coaching and also the steps I recommend to others.

1. Suspend Judgment.

     If you get more stubborn every time you are corrected, one day you will be crushed and never recover.
    P.S. 29:1 (GNT)

2. Write down the wise counsel. The process of writing down the coaching points will not only organize the thoughts in *your* mind, it will make it easier to do the next step.
3. Share what you wrote down. This not only confirms to your coach that you find their coaching helpful, it also makes sure you did, in fact, hear them correctly.
4. Thank them and *then* ask questions to clarify and get more coaching on the issues being discussed.
5. Agree on what, how and when decisions. Discuss *what* you are going to do differently as a result of the coaching; *what* you need to do to make these changes; *how* you are planning to make the changes or get the things you need to make the change; and *when* you will make the change. Be specific.

6. Finally, thank them for their help and decide on your next coaching session allowing you to remain accountable to your coach

Weigh the wise counsel – In the end, you are 100% accountable for the decisions you make in life. Weigh the counsel and determine for yourself what you are going to do.

> A king sitting as judge weighs all the evidence carefully, distinguishing the true from false.
> P.S. 20:8 (TLB)

Execute! Once a decision is made, the sales professional takes the wise counsel they have committed themselves to and follow through. One of the colors in the Sales Octane Values Flag is Red and it stands for our value, "I am 100% accountable." Red was chosen to reinforce the statement, "if you cut us...we bleed accountability!"

> Anyone who despises a word of advice will pay for it, but whoever heeds a command will be rewarded.
> P.S. 13:13 (ISV)

As you commit yourself to gaining wise counsel and being 100% accountable to execute, it will not take long and you will be the wise person, respected in your space and sought out by both customers and others. You will have moved from good to great and are about to dominate in a referral-based world.

> If you listen to correction to improve your life, you will be at home among the wise.
> P.S. 15:31 (NCV)(NLT)

Chapter 26
Organize

There is a structure to everything in the universe and the sales process is no exception. Random is not an option when it comes to the sales professional. In order to move from good to great we must have systems in place to drive success.

 Put your outdoor work in order. Get your fields ready. After that, build your house.
P.S. 24:27 (NIRV)

This sliver of timeless wisdom may not seem to apply in our current day and age. In sales, at best our "farming" is limited to our territory. The author is simply sharing the time-honored principle of putting order to our situation and approaching each step in order. First things first. If the farmer does not first establish order to his property then getting the fields ready is a mute point. Once the property is defined the fields can be prepared, tilled, and planted. Now there is a high probability of a harvest simply because they followed the first order of business. If the house was built first the farmer certainly would have a place to live, but since the fields were not prepared, tilled and planted in season there would be no harvest. The excitement of the new home would wear off in short order.

 Whoever works his farmland will have abundant food
P.S. 28:19a (ISV)

The sales professional understands the importance of putting a plan in place to create the conditions for growth, and then working the plan so there is a harvest year after year. The cycle of agriculture is a consistent cycle that cannot be manipulated. Sales is no different. So plan your work first, *then* work your plan.

The basics of networking must be in place at the start. Social Media sites, associations, groups, marketing automation, circles of influence and every new and emerging tool must be in place first. This form of organic-lead generation takes time, which is why it must be there before you get too far down the path. There are many great books and content experts on these strategies. For now, we will focus on the specific items the sales professional must put in place once they get a contact, name or lead.

Evaluate to Qualify

Time is the new currency for the sales professional just as it is for our customers. We must make sure we spend our time and resources on qualified opportunities. Having a system in place to qualify opportunities is essential. Especially when you understand that over 53% of the population is extroverted, and over 60% of salespeople jump way past the average in terms of extroversion and optimism. This translates to a desire to get excited about opportunities before they have been properly qualified.

Ideal Customer Profiling

The same way you would profile the ideal sales professional, you should profile the ideal customer. There are many variations of customer profiling available. At the very least, the profiling will include budget, size, industry, decision-making process, stakeholder access, decision maker identified, timing and challenges/needs aligned with your solution. The profiling may include geographic, demographic and psychographic criteria. The key is to develop a profile and then consistently evaluate the wins and losses against the profiling criteria. Once you create the list of criteria, you can create great questions to use earlier in process to qualify for your ideal customers.

Talk to any nutritionist and they will tell you to avoid grocery shopping when you are hungry. You will buy everything you see.

Someone who is full refuses honey, when you're starved, you could eat a horse.
P.S. 27:7 (CEB)(MSG)

This is the same reality with sales where the hungry salesperson, if not evaluating opportunities using the ideal customer profile, will spend their time on any opportunity, even unqualified ones.

If you are busy with unqualified opportunities, you will have less time to focus on the qualified ones. As the sales funnel narrows, you need to have the time and availability to work with the qualified lead that comes to you farther down the sales cycle. When you say no to unqualified opportunities, you say yes to qualified opportunities. Frankly, if they are unqualified they are not opportunities at all. They are fantasies.

The one who works his land will have plenty of food, but whoever chases fantasies lacks sense.
P.S. 12:11 (HCSB)

This is the second time where the author repeats himself. The first repetition involved the chattering fool and now it is the person that chases after fantasies. Pay attention. If we ask better questions, listen to the answers and then have the sense to make the right decision, we will focus on qualified opportunities and be able to give the prospect an exceptional experience.

> Whoever works his farmland will have abundant food,
> but whoever chases fantasies will become very poor.
> P.S. 28:19 (ISV)

There is an alternative, continue to go after unqualified opportunities but make no mistake, you will only suffer the consequences.

> The prudent person sees trouble ahead and hides,
> but the naïve continue on and suffer the consequences.
> P.S. 22:3 (ISV)

The prudent think of the long-term view. Focusing time on ideal customers will keep us out of trouble now and in the future.

> The wise [prudent] see trouble ahead and avoid it,
> but fools keep going and get into trouble
> P.S. 22:3 (EXB)

This is the third time the author repeats himself. Frankly, this is one of the most critical elements to sales success. ONLY spend your time on qualified opportunities because the prospective customer will listen once you are in front of them. Unqualified opportunities will not listen to you anyway and while you may be busy, it's a downward spiral. As you will not have time for qualified prospects.

When we focus our efforts on qualified opportunities, there is a greater probability the prospective customer will listen and engage with our offering.

> Don't speak to a foolish person.
> He will only ignore your wise words.
> P.S. 23:9 (ICB)

Efficient System to Drive Your Sales Activity

Are you focused on business or is it really just busy-ness? Too often we are so busy but much of this busy-ness (looks like Bus-i-ness) may be the result of spending time on fantasies. Once we focus on our ideal customer the next challenge is our own sales system.

Earlier, we discussed the ways in which the traditional sales funnel is becoming more like a large straw from Starbucks.

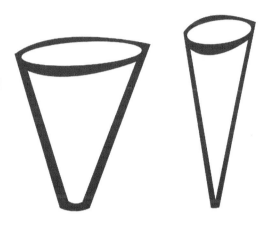

Our customers are experiencing the same exact situation we experience with them regarding the difficulty to forecast. They have very little view of the future. It's feast or famine and it changes on a dime. So, when you get the call from a qualified customer you need to be ready to go.

At the same time, this new dynamic results in projects being started and then put on hold. One day you get an urgent call and the qualified opportunity is back on. The question is, what system have you put in place to quickly gather their historical data and pick up right where you left off, efficiently?

Efficient Retrieval of Data Including Your Handwritten Notes

In the P.S. below, "Food," represents information and there are two elements to put in place: big data and your personal notes. We have already discussed using CRM for big data, so now it is down to you, the sales professional and your personal notes.

> Ants are not very strong.
> But they store up food in the summer.
> P.S. 30:25 (ICB)

Much of what the sales professional does is think. We are constantly thinking of great ideas to share with a customer, names of people to connect with; to-do's we cannot forget, great angles or strategies, the list is endless. These random thoughts often enter our mind, sparked by images and conversations, or they simply cycle through memory. Psychology of Selling Principle #18 talks about short-term memory. If we don't capture the thought quickly, it will be gone.

Think it, Ink it

The sales professional creates the discipline of writing thoughts down as soon as possible. Many sales professionals actually write things down and here lies the next problem. It is not uncommon to see sales professionals with tablets of legal paper scribbled with information. Sticky notes clutter their cars, offices and even dayplanners. Dayplanners look like the Encyclopedia Britannica. Journals, worthy of Hemingway, stuff their briefcases. Mobile devices with dictated or typed notes. But here's the problem: it's static.

Team

Team selling requires shared information. As you engage with customers much of the information you write down needs to be shared on a broad platform with your team members, and the sooner, the better. But the information is static so back to the office, transcribe those notes into the CRM, email, or shared drive. With each translation something is lost and I am not just talking about your time or potentially, the opportunity.

Sanity

A major source of anxiety is the question, "where did I write that down?" or, "where did I put that?" In most cases, "that" are the notes you have been writing, dictating or typing.

Time

Sales is hard work and you need down time. The clutter of sales begins to creep into our personal time much like lava, slow, nearly indiscernible, and before long you are burned out. Personal time aside, even if you are able to transcribe and move your notes around during business hours you are duplicating the effort. You wrote the note down once. Why do you have to write it on another page of your dayplanner, or pull it off the legal pad and write it on another document, or copy and paste it to another media? Static information no longer works for the sales professional.

Life

Try as you might, you cannot separate personal from business. The separation passed years ago when we combined personal and business by carrying our phone with us everywhere. My goal in life is to help you get your life back and sell a lot in the process.

This is our new reality, and if you play it right, you will improve your results and get more time. You are in the grocery store picking up a few things and you suddenly have a great idea regarding a customer. You have two options. You could write it down or try to remember it. If you try to remember it, you will likely forget it. The sales professional is always thinking and as a result they are (or should be) always inking! So you wrote your idea down while in the store. Excellent! The fact remains, the note you just scribbled or dictated is static.

Digital vs. Analog (paper)

How do you improve your results, get more time and navigate the personal and business life challenge. It's not hard.

As the sales process incorporates more mobile applications the answer is right around the corner. We get excited about showing our customers pictures, videos or specifications right on our mobile device. Nice. We plug in specifications and information on our mobile device to speed up order entry and eliminate duplication. Good. Why not take it one more step and throw away your dayplanner, your legal pads, your leather journals and your sticky notes? Think digital all the way and you will never go astray. This is how the sales professional moves from Good to Great.

	Paper & Pen	Computer/Tablet with Keyboard	Digital Handwriting App
Searchable		✓	✓
Portability		✓	✓
Backed Up		✓	✓
Easily Shared		✓	✓
Engages Customer	✓		✓
Integrates Images		✓	✓
Large Amount Captured	✓		✓

Digital *handwritten* notes are a key step in building out your sales system.

Paper and pen are great for engaging with your customer. The customer sees you writing and they know you are engaged. Paper and pen are great for capturing large amounts of information as the customer opens up with you. The problem is you cannot integrate images, photos, etc. You cannot share the information with your team members or customers easily or efficiently. You cannot back up your notes easily or efficiently. The notes are not portable, meaning they are not on multiple platforms, not easily searched and not easily transferred to their next step (CRM, task list, client file, etc.). Worse, they are not backed up to the cloud.

If you have already moved on to a computer or a tablet with a keyboard, you now have the ability to integrate images, easily share data, back up data and have even become portable. However, unless you are a speed typist, a large amount of the customer's information could remain uncaptured. The other issue becomes how dramatically reduced our engagement is with the customer. We have all been there when someone whips out their digital device and begins tapping on the keyboard like a chimpanzee. Not sure about you, but my first thought is, "why are you checking email/social media?" Not great for a first impression.

Digital note taking applications bring everything together. You can write everything you are already writing in your day planner, legal pads, leather journals and sticky notes. For those of you who like to dictate using voice recognition, you can continue that process right into the digital note application. It's just like writing so the customer sees you are engaged with what they are saying. You can import photos, images and documents, even forms.

You are able to share information with your team and customers immediately. It is backed up within seconds of you writing the note. It is portable, meaning you can easily access the information on other platforms. It is searchable, so you will never spend time wondering where you wrote it. And, best of all, it is easily transferred to the next step (CRM, task list, client file, etc.).

When the customer is ready to engage, you already have the details from every conversation in your hand. Intelligent and dynamic.

Get it Out of Your Mind

You can organize your strategy much faster once you get it from your mind to paper. Once you get it out of your mind on the digital paper you can look at it, others can look at it, and you can improve the strategy. More eyes equal more ideas. Even better, you will not have to erase and re-write, it's digital. For the first time ever, you will not spend time worrying about where things are or how you are going to find the time to share it with others.

And it Gets Better

- Take all the questions you created with your Ideal Customer Profile and put them on your digital note application.
- Put your pre-call research steps on your digital note application.
- Put your pre-call plan steps on your digital note application.
- Put every question you would ask, by solution, in your digital note application.

Now you are organized for the incoming call, the first connection and every situation! Backed up, searchable, portable, mobile, easy to share and visual. Or you could keep writing on paper.

Chapter 27
Plan Your Work

Most top-level decision makers share a common behavioral style. We train sales professionals to engage with top-level decision makers using three steps:
- Be brief.
- Be bright (relevant).
- Be gone.

When you show up with great questions, all relevant because of the pre-call research you performed, capture all of the customer's notes using the digital note taking application, and have a plan on how to move the sale forward to the next step, another aspect of your pre-call plan, you will be brief, bright and gone. The top-level decision maker will love you.

The Brain Works Faster than the Mouth

If the salesperson is trying to think of the next question or step they are not listening to the customer. Contrary to ideas of "multi-tasking" you cannot do two things at the same time. When you are engaged with the customer you must have 80% of your questions and steps defined as you head into the conversation. The remaining 20% will be the new information you gain that drives additional questions or insight that you have not heard before. The new reality is you will constantly update your questions and insights in your digital note application for the next customer.

Moving Forward

The number one complaint I hear from sales managers when asked how their teams need to improve is how their sales people plan to move the sale forward. This is one key element of your pre-call research and is often referred to as the next step.

It is difficult to be in control of something you have not thought about prior to the conversation. With the pre-call plan on your digital note taking application you will have the time-honored transition statements you have previously used to move the sale forward available before the appointment. You just need to select the one most appropriate and have it in front of you and you are set.

 Careful planning puts you ahead in the long run; hurry and scurry puts you further behind.
P.S. 21:5 (MSG)

Don't Let Planning Become Procrastination

The reason for procrastination, in part, is fear and also poor time management. The fear of rejection causes us to stay in the safety of pre-call research/planning to avoid the possibility of making the call and being rejected. The other issue is time management. The salesperson is too busy to take the time to efficiently and effectively complete their planning. The digital note taking application aids in being more effective and more efficient. The final piece is leveraging Parkinson's Law.

WORK EXPANDS SO AS TO FILL THE TIME AVAILABLE FOR ITS COMPLETION.
- C. Northcote Parkinson

Think about how you work on the days leading up to vacation. Your focus is amazing. The reason is you are leveraging Parkinson's Law. The time available cannot expand because you have a date to leave on vacation so the work can not expand beyond that date.

Follow the same principle with every activity such as pre-call research, pre-call planning and any other routine task you undertake as a sales professional. Set a duration of time or a deadline for each task and you will move faster, and make that call.

Let's look back to Groundhog Day. The lesson is to apply what you learn and to incorporate those changes into your system in an effort to continuously improve. Learn from yours and others mistakes and best practices, and when you Think It, Ink It!

One Spot = Efficient/Effective/Sanity – Everything, business and personal, needs to go into your CRM/Note application. This is not a sign of weakness. You can turn it off whenever you want, but it is always with you when you need it. Become disciplined to move everything to one spot and everything gets better.

Redundant = Recurring – Everything you do redundantly needs to become a recurring entry in your CRM or checklist in your digital note taking application. This is good for a couple of reasons. First, you don't have to spend a lot of time or anxiety trying to remember when you did something last, whether you have it down or what you need to do. And second, as you look at your calendar or checklist, you see what you have to do and you will not overcommit. When we don't overcommit we are able to do what we said we would do.

Repetition = Clicks – One click away is your goal. If you have to retype things three to four times in an email there is a problem with the system. Copying and pasting takes too long. Create the dropdown menus and watch your productivity soar.

A simple man believes anything
(including that they will win without a plan)
But a prudent man gives thought to his steps
P.S. 14:15 (NIV)

We deceive ourselves when activity feels like productivity. The sales professional plans their work. They evaluate where they spend their time with a system that is efficient, engaged and effective. The last step is to Execute.

The wisdom of the prudent is to give thoughts to their ways,
but the folly of fools is deception
P.S. 14:8 (NIV)

Chapter 28
Work Your Plan

Once you have put your system in place and organized your plan, the final step is to work the plan, as in execute.

SALES IS THE EASIEST LOW-PAYING JOB.
SALES IS THE HARDEST HIGH-PAYING JOB.

Sales is hard work as you put the system in place and consistently and persistently execute the steps. It's like the merry-go-round we spoke of earlier. A lot of work to get it going, but after it's moving, it takes less effort to keep it going.

You may be a business owner, or perhaps you are an entrepreneur reading this book. You understand the drive required when working for yourself. For sales professionals employed by a company, I want you to think the same way, as if it is your company, because, in reality, it is. You are the owner of ME, Inc., because once you enter sales you truly are self-employed!

<u>Get Going</u>

> You lazy people can learn by watching an anthill.
> Ants don't have leaders,
> but they store up food during harvest season.
> P.S. 6:6-8 (CEV)

We have all been there. Vacation. As the days of vacation go by, we tend to sleep in a little later and become more and more relaxed. That is just fine when on vacation. However, it is a habit and the same way it takes time on vacation to sleep in later, the sales professional needs to have the habit of rising early!

> As a door turns on its hinges,
> so the lazy person turns on his bed.
> P.S. 26:14 (GW)

The word picture is brilliant. A door moving on a hinge is no different than the motion of the lazy person in bed. The next time you feel the urge to "roll over" and hit the snooze button remember this. Get up early.

> If you are lazy and sleep your time away,
> you will starve.
> P.S. 19:15 (CEV)

> A little sleep, a little slumber,
> a little folding of the arms to rest
> P.S. 6:10 & 24:33 (NABRE)

This is the fourth of only five times in 915 situations where the timeless-wisdom repeats itself. Notice what this is not about. It is not about a frantic pace of work. It is not about working every day, holidays and weekends. It is not about working every waking hour. It is about little increments. Tiny habits. It would appear from the use of the word little, as in little sleep, or little slumber, or a little folding of the hands to rest, that the writer is not talking about a massive difference but rather a little something extra. It's the tiny habits.

While the saying a little sleep, a little slumber, a little folding of the arms to rest is repeated twice, in each case there is a slightly different observation that precedes the call for tiny habits.

> How long, O sluggard, will you lie there?
> when will you rise from your sleep?
> P.S. 6:9 (NABRE)

The first is simply the question of how long will you lie there?

As I gazed at it, I reflected;
I saw and learned a lesson: When will you get up from your sleep?"
P.S. 24:32 (NABRE)

The other is the lesson learned with the question. Clearly both are admonishment for the person who sleeps in and starts their day late. This is pretty simple to understand. Bottom line, get going early. You decide what early is but clearly it's before your competitors get going. And it is the same net result with a little sleep, a little slumber and a little folding of the hands.

Suddenly poverty hits you and everything is gone!
P.S. 24:34 & 6:11 (CEV)

WORK Diligently

The sales professional is diligent with every step in the sales process. It takes diligent work to put the system in place, learn the new skills, attend the networking events, do the research, plan the calls, make the calls, overcome rejections, remain relevant, ask great questions, say no to unqualified opportunities, do what you say you will do every step along the way, and start the process all over again each day. Even after a great day, quarter or year you still go from heroes to zeros and start over. It's the nature of sales.

The diligent find freedom in their work;
the lazy are oppressed by work.
P.S. 12:24 (MSG)

Working diligently is what differentiates the sales professional from the others. If it were easy, anyone could do it. Remain diligent and eventually you will get a break. It is the way it works for the sales professional.

 Unrelenting disappointment leaves you heartsick, but a sudden good break can turn life around.
P.S. 13:12 (MSG)

When you work diligently it may be the next call that is the start of the change. Oftentimes you hear others suggest luck is involved when the break comes.

> I AM A GREAT BELIEVER IN LUCK, AND I FIND THE HARDER I WORK, THE MORE I HAVE OF IT.
> - Thomas Jefferson

Put another way, the harder I work the luckier I get! As any business owner will tell you, there is no such thing as luck. Welcome to ME, Inc.

WORK Towards Perfection

Years ago I worked with someone who always responded to the question, "How are you?" with the statement, "Nearly perfect!" The goal of the sales professional is to get as close to perfection as possible. Rather than simply meeting the expectations of others, the sales professional strives to exceed expectations. This is accomplished by avoiding over-commitments.

When you over-commit you set yourself up to under-perform. When you manage your commitments you set yourself up to exceed the customer's expectations. It is easy to over-commit in your desire to please your customer. But in the end, both lose.

You miss your commitment and the customer misses their next step in the process predicated on your date.

It is far easier to take the high road and manage the expectations.

> **WELL DONE IS BETTER THAN WELL SAID**
> - Benjamin Franklin

Talk and Try Go Hand in Hand

There is a lot of talk in the sales profession. Talk about our plans, talk about the calls we are going to make, talk about how we are going to learn and practice and improve. But talk will only take us so far. Eventually we will have to work hard if we plan to be successful.

> Those who work hard make a profit.
> But those who only talk will be poor.
> P.S. 14:23 (ICB)

In one of the early Star War movies there was a scene with Luke Skywalker, the young apprentice and Yoda, his coach. In response to a recommendation from Yoda, Luke commented, "OK, I'll try." Yoda immediately snapped back "NO! Do. Or do not. There is no try." It's true. Nothing gets accomplished unless we do something. Mere talk will only take us so far. Nothing is accomplished until we do.

> **DO. OR DO NOT. THERE IS NO TRY!**
> - Yoda

WORK Together

Sales is a team sport and whether you have a team or simply work with others in your company you must set the work ethic. If you are slack in your work, the rest of the team will follow suit. If you establish a strong work ethic, others will see your commitment and rise to the occasion.

> One who is slack in his work is brother to him who is a master of destruction.
> P.S. 18:9 (WEB)

When you are placed in a situation where you lead a sales team *without* management authority, it is even more important to lead by example. If this is the case, the only reason the team would follow you is if they believe in you. Lead by example and watch them move in formation alongside you. There is nothing like leading by example.

> While locusts live without a ruler, they all *know how to* move in formation;
> P.S. 30:27 (VOICE)

WORK without Fear

There is an endless stream of challenges with the sales process; Competition, economics, technologies, markets, products and services are a few challenges the sales professional faces. Realistically, none of them will be as bad as predicted. Bad news sells, and for whatever reason, we are drawn to it. The sales professional is aware of what is going on, puts things into perspective, and controls what they have the power to control.

The sales professional works without fear and leaves looking over the shoulder to the competition. Fear is the most common emotion separating the sales professional from the rest of the pack. The sales professional must learn to overcome their fears as they move from good to great. The sales professional does not spend time looking over their shoulder at all the things others fear, they simply keep moving forward in confidence.

The worries of the sluggard are typically very misplaced. Look above at the words of the slug. Lions don't hang out in the streets of a city. The chances of attack are remote. What is really happening here? Easy, the sluggard is simply looking for a reason to stay in bed and stay inside versus getting up and out.

The sluggard spends their time looking for reasons not to put together the plan, not to execute the plan, not to learn new skills and not to hit their goals. They just love to talk about things other than themselves to take the focus off their poor results. It is always something or someone else.

The mind cannot tell the difference between reality and what it is being told. So what are you telling your mind? Dr. David Thompson, in his book, *Whatever You Fear is Who You Are*, talks about the importance of facing your fears lest you become the very thing you are avoiding. Knowing yourself, fears included, is the first step in becoming a sales professional. You need to know your fears and confront them. If not, then as Thompson's book suggests, you will ultimately become the very thing you fear.

If we fear rejection, common for a certain set of salespeople, then if left un-confronted, we will ultimately experience rejection. Here's an example of how it works. We don't make a lot of prospecting calls because we fear rejection. When we don't make a lot of prospecting calls, we don't hit our goals, when we don't hit our goals, we don't make money. When we don't make money, we face, you got it, rejection.

You are who you are and the sooner you identify your fears you can begin the process of improvement. The sales professional does not allow themselves to live in denial!

It is helpful to remember it's never as bad as what you think it will be, and If you don't overcome your fear then you will increase the probability of experiencing a negative result. Facing your fear presents opportunity to overcome your fear and ultimately experience growth!

WORK Your Numbers

In the same way there were tiny habits with the sleep, slumber and folding of the hands, there is the same reality when it comes to our numbers. The sales professional is always watching their numbers to look for trends. When the numbers are trending in the right direction, keep moving. However, when things are trending in the wrong direction don't go into denial. It takes effort to build a sales pipeline but very little effort to watch it evaporate.

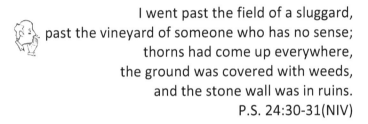

> I went past the field of a sluggard,
> past the vineyard of someone who has no sense;
> thorns had come up everywhere,
> the ground was covered with weeds,
> and the stone wall was in ruins.
> P.S. 24:30-31(NIV)

Think about it this way. How much effort is involved in establishing a vineyard with a stone wall around the premises? A lot of work. How much effort is required to let the weeds and thorns overtake the vineyard and the stone wall to begin to fall apart? No work at all. Just stop doing what needs to be done and it overtakes you in a short period of time. Work your numbers and watch the trends

WORK Upright, Take the "High"way

Everyone, including me, wants to work fast. If I can get something done in half the time why would I not do it? When we work smart and hard, we put ourselves on a highway where we can move along at a faster pace.

 The way of the sluggard is blocked with thorns, but the path of the upright is a highway.
P.S. 15:19 (NIV)

The word picture is great. Working upright puts us on a highway.

HIGHWAY   PATH

Many years ago I was a road warrior so I know the characteristics of a highway. Recently I purchased a mountain bike, a Surly Pugsley, so I know the characteristics of a thorny path. I must have read this Proverbial Saying (P.S.) a dozen times and then started drawing the images on my light-board.

Let's say you were *not on vacation* and the challenge in front of you was simply to travel 100 miles and the goal was to get there as quickly as possible. If you had the option of taking the highway or taking a path, which would you take? Most likely, you would take the highway.

Straight, more direct route to your destination.

HIGHWAY   PATH

START   START

FINISH   FINISH

Less obstacles to work around and avoid.

Well marked. You know where you are headed and there are far fewer spontaneous decisions to make.

The bumps and dips are leveled out meaning far less wear and tear on you!

And it's faster, legally!

When you get on the highway you simply move faster toward your destination and arrive earlier, well ahead of the competition.

On the "path", however, obstructions, delays, etc. are the RULE; thorns, overgrowth, rocks, sticks, unchartered territory, things above and things below. There are challenges with each situation but with the highway obstructions are consistently less!

So what does it mean when it says "upright?" What is upright? It's not simply being UP and out of bed. It's all the characteristics we covered earlier.

Honesty, humility, generosity, patience, self-control, speech, listening and likability are all elements of integrity and all required as we move in the direction from good to great.

We move in this direction as we invest in knowledge and wise counsel.

As we expand our connections our reputation and our reach grows.

As we organize and plan our work we position ourselves to become effective and efficient.

Then, we work our plan, consistently and persistently. Soon the path turns into a highway and we speed along arriving sooner at our destination.

The sales professional who is highly referable is now positioned to leverage a referral-based world. And it all begins with timeless wisdom.

Chapter 29
Next Step

So, where do we start?

1. Systems, 2. Team, 3. Practice, 4. Execute, 5. Evaluate

> Easy come, easy go,
> but steady diligence pays off.
> P.S. 13:11 (MSG)

This will take work. When we structure the systems, hire the right people, practice, execute, evaluate our results and adjust, the sales process can be a lot of fun.

> Do not wear yourself out to get rich.
> Have the wisdom to show restraint.
> P.S. 23:4 (NIV)

There are six colors in the Sales Octane values flag. The last color is orange. Orange is bright, orange is fun, orange makes me smile. The color orange stands for our value we have fun! If the journey is not fun, what's the use?

We will make this journey a lot of fun!

You have my word,

Jim Ryerson
Chief Acceleration Officer
Sales Octane, Inc.

> One last P.S. - Let's go!
> Make hay while the sun shines—that's smart;
> P.S. 10:5 (MSG)

Thank you!

Jane, thanks for keeping me on task these past 33.5 years! I am so blessed to be able to have you in my life! Thanks to Kate, Ryan, Elizabeth and Anna as each of you illustrate timeless wisdom every day.

Scott, thanks for keeping all the details straight so I can focus on my unique ability. I could not have done this book without you!

> As iron sharpens iron,
> so people can improve each other.
> P.S. 27:17 (EXB)

So many people gave me ideas, insight, counsel and correction during the first iteration of this book. In alphabetical order: Ryan Anderson, Dave Brandsen, Jim Bush, Wayne Breitbarth, Lance Chisum, David Cummings, Simon De Groot, Katie Delaney, Whitney DeVos, Jacob Dunlap, Seth Gamblin, Dan Gish, Terri Grady, Todd James, Craig Johnson, Mark Johnson, Tim Kleyn, Jeff Manion, Chris McMorrow, Tom Palumbo, Fred Reichheld, Scott Riffel, Tim Sanders, Edward Waller and Tom Zbikowski. If I missed you, please call me!

And without the teams at Apple Joint Venture, Atlanta Tech Village, Bible Gateway, Notes Plus and Target Training International this would have taken even longer to complete.

> Without counsel plans fail,
> but with many advisers they succeed.
> P.S. 15:22 (ESVUK)

References

In an effort to make the content of this book easily understood I used a multitude of translations. Listed below are the translations along with the reference code used in Selling by the BOOK Today.

(CEB) Common English Bible
Copyright © 2011 by Common English Bible

(CEV) Contemporary English Version
Copyright © 1995 by American Bible Society

(CJB) Complete Jewish Bible
Copyright © 1998 by David H. Stern. All rights reserved.

(ERV) Easy-to-Read Version
Copyright © 2006 by World Bible Translation Center

(ESVUK) English Standard Version Anglicised
The Holy Bible, English Standard Version Copyright © 2001 by Crossway Bibles, a division of Good News Publishers.

(EXB) Expanded Bible
The Expanded Bible, Copyright © 2011 Thomas Nelson Inc. All rights reserved.

(GNT) Good News Translation
Copyright © 1992 by American Bible Society

(GW) GOD'S WORD Translation Copyright © 1995 by God's Word to the Nations. Used by permission of Baker Publishing Group

(HCSB) Holman Christian Standard Bible
Copyright © 1999, 2000, 2002, 2003, 2009 by Holman Bible Publishers, Nashville Tennessee. All rights reserved.

(ICB) The Holy Bible, International Children's Bible, Copyright © 2015 Thomas Nelson Inc. All rights reserved.

(ISV) International Standard Version
Copyright © 1995-2014 by ISV Foundation. ALL RIGHTS RESERVED INTERNATIONALLY. Used by permission of Davidson Press, LLC.

(KJ21) 21st Century King James Version
Copyright © 1994 by Deuel Enterprises, Inc.

(KJV) King James Version
by Public Domain

(MSG) The Message
Copyright © 1993, 1994, 1995, 1996, 2000, 2001, 2002 by Eugene H. Peterson

(NABRE) New American Bible, revised edition
© 2010, 1991, 1986, 1970 Confraternity of Christian Doctrine, Inc., Washington, DC All Rights Reserved.

(NASB) New American Standard Bible
Copyright © 1960, 1962, 1963, 1968, 1971, 1972, 1973, 1975, 1977, 1995 by The Lockman Foundation

(NCV) New Century Version
The Holy Bible, New Century Version®. Copyright © 2005 by Thomas Nelson, Inc.

(NIRV) New International Reader's Version
Copyright © 1995, 1996, 1998, 2014 by Biblica, Inc.®. Used by permission. All rights reserved worldwide.

(NIV) New International Version
Holy Bible, New International Version®, NIV® Copyright © 1973, 1978, 1984, 2011 by Biblica, Inc.® Used by permission. All rights reserved worldwide.

(NIVUK) New International Version - UK

Holy Bible, New International Version® Anglicized, NIV® Copyright © 1979, 1984, 2011 by HYPERLINK Biblica, Inc.® Used by permission. All rights reserved worldwide.

(NLT) New Living Translation
Holy Bible. New Living Translation copyright© 1996, 2004, 2007, 2013 by Tyndale House Foundation. Used by permission of Tyndale House Publishers Inc., Carol Stream, Illinois 60188. All rights reserved.

(NOG) Names of God Bible
The Names of God Bible (without notes) © 2011 by Baker Publishing Group.

(NRSVA) New Revised Standard Version, Anglicised
New Revised Standard Version Bible: Anglicised Edition, copyright © 1989, 1995 the Division of Christian Education of the National Council of the Churches of Christ in the United States of America. Used by permission. All rights reserved.

(TLB) Living Bible
The Living Bible copyright © 1971 by Tyndale House Foundation. Used by permission of Tyndale House Publishers Inc., Carol Stream, Illinois 60188. All rights reserved.

(VOICE) The Voice
The Voice Bible Copyright © 2012 Thomas Nelson, Inc. The Voice™ translation © 2012 Ecclesia Bible Society All rights reserved.

(WEB) World English Bible
by Public Domain. The name "World English Bible" is trademarked.

Made in the USA
Charleston, SC
09 December 2015